In Praise of Simplicity offers a vivid, thoughtful, and inspiring picture of the real life of a medical missionary to the Congo (and more briefly Liberia) over many years. We need to ground theorizing about mission in such long-term experience. Encounters with famous missionary predecessors, details of the demands of tropical medicine, danger, reflections of money and family, as well as the light of Scripture, are inter spliced in this well-written work. Wood is, in slang, the 'real deal,' and I commend his book.

Dr. George Sumner, *principal emeritus of Wycliffe College,*
Episcopal bishop of Dallas

I was privileged to know Philip Wood at Cambridge as a man whose deep Christian commitment was unquestionable. This book is an eminently readable and thought-provoking account of the way in which that commitment led him and his wife to serve God as medical missionaries in Africa. Philip introduces us to several journeys simultaneously – he takes us on a cultural journey laced with fascinating facts about the flora, fauna, people and customs he encounters. He also takes us on a medical journey that records his impressive ingenuity as he (often cheerfully) makes do with the minimum of surgical equipment in the most challenging of situations. He shares his passion for medical education, especially that of nurses. Most importantly he takes us on a spiritual and moral journey as he thinks through the implications of what he learns in light of biblical teaching. In the spirit of Georg Muller he calls Christian believers to think about what it means to trust God for all of life's circumstances and to be stewards of resources in the midst of extreme poverty and deprivation.

Dr. J.C. Lennox, *Professor of Mathematics, University of Oxford,*
Fellow in Mathematics and Philosophy of Science, Green Templeton College

Doctors Philip and Nancy Wood spent 40 years serving the people of war-torn Africa, practicing surgery and medicine. Their life-work included teaching and training more than a thousand nurses and doctors in the Democratic Republic of Congo. In September 2002 towards the end of the ten year D.R.C. civil war that claimed 4 million lives, Dr Philip Wood himself came to within an ace of losing his own life.

This record of sacrificial service in obedience to the call of Christ is told with self-effacing modesty, captivating clarity and illuminating insight. The details of daily life draw us into a world utterly different from what most of us ever experience. Below-the-surface cultural, ethical, political and relational issues are explored as they emerge.

The title *In Praise of Simplicity* is significant. Running through the book is the ever-present contrast between the abundance of material wealth and technological sophistication of the West, with the material poverty and yet relational richness of African communities. Coupled with this reality are reflections on the teaching of Jesus as recorded by Dr. Luke, about money, security, and where our hearts need to be. These searching observations do not leave us unmoved.

This is certainly a book of high adventure – flying in a single engine plane into a remote dirt airstrip to do days of surgery in unbelievably primitive conditions, calling for brilliant and ingenious improvisation. We travel with Philip on equally intrepid journeys, crossing crocodile-infested rivers on flimsy single lane log bridges, to bring life saving surgery and medicine to those who otherwise would die.

This is the account of two doctors deliberately choosing a life where material rewards were minimal, and where hardship, suffering, and danger was maximal. Ever present in this account is the undeniable and transforming reality of the love, comfort, miraculous provision, protection, and all sufficiency of the great God they served.

Canon Robin Guinness, *Toronto, Canada*

In Praise of Simplicity

A memoir of Christian service in times of peace and war in Africa

Dr. Philip B. Wood

In Praise of Simplicity

A memoir of Christian service in times of peace and war in Africa

Dr. Philip B. Wood

85 Miller Dr.
Ancaster, ON
Canada L9G 2H9

www.alevbooks.com

ISBN: 979-0-9881252-8-5

To my many friends and former students in the
Democratic Republic of Congo

Contents

Introduction 9

Chapter 1:   Emmanuel College, Cambridge 11
               Excursion 1: Dr. Luke and the Evidence 20

Chapter 2:   Bulstrode Manor, Gerrards Cross, Near London 22
               Excursion 2: The "Life of Faith" 31

Chapter 3:   Centre d'Accueil Protestant (CAP), Kinshasa, Congo 36
               Excursion 3: Healthy relationships are the key to
               true wealth 40

Chapter 4:   Centre Médical Évangélique, Nyankunde 43
               Excursion 4: "Blessed are the poor for theirs is the
               kingdom of God" 50

Chapter 5:   Travels in the Garden of Eden 54
               Excursion 5: "What shall we do then?" 69

Chapter 6:   Snapshots 72
               Excursion 6: "The Love of Money" 84

Chapter 7:   Liberian Labor 87
               Excursion 7: "Laying Up Treasures in Heaven" 93

Chapter 8:   Canadian interlude 96
               Excursion 8: On Persistent Prayer 101

Chapter 9:   Warfare and Wrecking 105
               Excursion 9: "Serving As Sheep Among Wolves" 111

Chapter 10:   Rebuilding 114
               Excursion 10: The Sin of Indifference 121

Chapter 11:   Retirement 126
               Excursion 11: Eternity Can Be Lonely 128

Chapter 12:   To Conclude... 131

Introduction

I LIKE TO THINK of myself as a well qualified general surgeon who was endlessly criticized for "burying himself"—or at any rate proposing to bury himself—in the heart of Africa. Was it worthwhile? That you will have to decide for yourself after having read this book. Was it fun? Most certainly! The travel, the friends made, the people ministered to, have made my career both very interesting and very fulfilling!

Perhaps the most important question I want to try and answer is, "Who paid your salary, and did it come regularly?" The answer: I went out with my wife believing that God would provide in accordance with the many instructions and promises that He gave his disciples as they set out on their own missionary careers. Over the years we discovered that He keeps His promises. It has not always been easy. Running a sophisticated medical centre in one of the poorest countries of the world, not having the necessary means to save someone's life when elsewhere you know you could, being confronted by corruption at every level, even within a Christian organization, being caught up in a war and, finally, rebuilding afterwards is not easy.

I have been most encouraged and influenced by the things which Dr. Luke chose to include in his gospel. He recorded numerous profound promises which, if you really believed them, would radically change your life-style. Usually I have not chosen to test those promises deliberately. However, I have found myself in situations where I had no choice but to take them literally. After telling my story I will include short "excursions" on a passage in Luke that relates to my experience. I hope that, as a result, you will be encouraged to delve deeper into the gospel of Luke and, above all, that you will be moved to a deeper trust in and experience of God.

My prayer is that the lessons I have learnt will encourage you to trust God more, will enable you to live free of anxiety about what lies around the corner, and that you will experience peace in this very troubled world—a peace that may be difficult to explain to others, or even to understand yourself, but a peace, a "shalom", that comes directly from God.

1

Emmanuel College, Cambridge

THERE IS A MYTH that states that all you need to do to obtain a Cambridge degree is eat dinner "in hall" five nights a week and then pass the exams. Attendance is not kept at lectures, and there may be little follow up if you fail to submit assignments. Attendance at dinner, however, was required. Dinner was quite an occasion. We would stand in our short undergraduate gowns round ancient oaken tables while the Master and Fellows processed in from the senior parlour to take their places around the elevated head table. This was followed by a lengthy Latin prayer, after which we could sit down to savour a three course meal.

Wow! The previous week I'd been a mere schoolboy, and now a naïve undergraduate being addressed as "Sir", and waited on by the porters of the College. In theory we would mix with students of different disciplines around the dinner table so that our erudite conversations would broaden our education. I, for the life of me, cannot remember many "erudite conversations"; the skill of carrying on a conversation was one element of my schoolboy makeup that matured rather slowly.

My initial reaction to being at Cambridge was a mixture of pride in being there in the first place, as well as of appreciation of the institution's architecture and gardens, its history and unique customs: every morning a "bedder" would clean my room and make my bed!

Suggesting that dinners and exams were all one needed to worry about is, indeed, a myth. We medical students were given a "grey book" which needed to be filled with an array of dazzling signatures from all our teachers at every stage of our education before we would be graced with the label "doctor".

Most lectures and some labs were held in the mornings, while other labs and seminars needed to be fitted in either in the afternoons or evenings. Basically, one needed to work every afternoon to get the evening off, or every evening if you played sports in the afternoon. To excel at a sport, particularly a team sport—and specifically rowing—was seen as the ideal partner to an Englishman's academic development. A first class degree and a "blue" for playing against Oxford was perceived as the highest honour Cambridge could bestow. However, many of us opted to drop sports in order to take advantage of the many other evening activities, such as the Cambridge Union debates or the College Musical Society's lectures and concerts.

If dining "in hall" was an inspiring event, the anatomy dissecting room came as a huge shock for which this schoolboy was totally unprepared. The place was full of naked formalized (embalmed) human bodies. We were assigned in pairs to learn the structure of the human body by dissecting all the different parts during our two years of anatomy studies, much as medical students have done since antiquity. These days, 3D imagery is improving the teaching of human anatomy, and less people are willing to offer their bodies to science. Even with a body in front of me I found anatomy difficult; I have a lot of sympathy for African medical students who have to learn this basic science of medicine with just a blackboard and a piece of chalk, and with the aid of a professor who may not himself have a good grasp of the finer details of the human body!

The genius of a Cambridge education lies in its seminar system. Each week we had a seminar of one hour with one of the lecturers or a PhD student in each of the three subjects we were taking that year, along with just two or at most three other undergraduates. A Dr. Titchen was my seminar tutor in physiology, the study of the function of the body. His gruff exterior and demanding assignments scared many, including myself initially, but I came to appreciate his efforts at encouraging us to seriously and scientifically think about the subject. One important lesson he taught me was to "know the facts but doubt conclusions". The gruesome illustration he gave us of this principle was the sectioning of the brain of an anaesthetized cat. As you section the brain from the front towards the back the cat will become completely paralysed at a certain point. Some might then conclude that they have therefore discovered the level in the brain that instigates movement. Not according to Dr. Titchen: "You have done such a crude experiment with so many uncontrolled elements that the only conclusion that you can draw is that when you cut an anaesthetized cat at that level he becomes paralyzed." Dr. Titchen's suspicion of conclusions has helped me as a scientist to correlate Biblical truth with our scientific exploration of the universe. I firmly believe God created both His word and the universe, and that any apparent contradictions stem from wrong conclusions on one side or the other.

I later learnt, unofficially, that I could have been awarded a first class degree at the discretion of the examiners. My physiology grade was excellent, but a poor showing in anatomy pulled me down. Fortunately I did far better when I had to relearn anatomy during surgical training; by that time I had a much better idea about the practical application of this knowledge in medicine.

Although my parents had brought me up as a Christian, it was at university that I made the Christian faith my own. Stepping out into the world allowed me to question the principles I had absorbed from my family background. When I first arrived at Cambridge there was a fellowship of Christians, the SCM, which held to a more liberal approach to the Christian faith and the Bible. They, however, folded during my first year and a number of their remaining members joined the Cambridge Inter-Collegiate Christian Union (CICCU).

I found the CICCU (precursor of the Intervarsity Christian Fellowship, now the Universities and Colleges Christian Fellowship) enormously stimulating and encouraging. On Saturday evenings, week after week, the best Bible expositors in the land came to interact with Cambridge students in the Union building. About a tenth of the undergraduate body (about 1000 students of the 9000 undergraduates at the time) would meet in the debating chamber for a Bible exposition given by one of these preachers. They came in part because the CICCU could invite and choose the best Christian teachers in the country—and these men invariably accepted the invitation. We heard John Stott, Martin Lloyd Jones, Dick Lucas, Leon Morris and many others. They would teach on Saturday evening, preach in one of the Cambridge churches the next morning, and then give an evangelistic message in Holy Trinity church – Simeon's old church – on Sunday evening.

Charles Simeon was appointed to Holy Trinity in 1782 against the wishes of the church wardens and congregation. They disliked his earnest manner and evangelical messages. When he proposed starting an evening service the wardens actually locked the church doors on him.

This kind of opposition continued for a number of years, but he never gave up, and gradually the response to his ministry was so encouraging that he erected a gallery in the south transept at his own expense. He ended his life as the best known 'character' in Cambridge, his funeral in Kings College Chapel attended by some two thousand people.

No less important than the talks were the coffee hours we organized back in Emmanuel College after the Saturday evening studies. That was when we explored the implications of what we had heard though, at times, our more esoteric discussions were distracted by the young women who joined us from Homerton Teacher's Training College, or the nurses from Addenbrooks Hospital.

During my second year at Cambridge we celebrated the 150th anniversary of the Daily Prayer Meeting. For 150 years a group of Cambridge students had been gathering at 1 PM to pray for the needs of Cambridge and the world. How does one celebrate such an important anniversary? It was eventually agreed that we would, well, have a prayer meeting! I was asked to organize a small group to pray for Southern Sudan. The civil war there was intensifying, and Christian work was being disrupted by an increasing Muslim influence from the north. The research I did for that prayer meeting vastly increased my hitherto miniscule knowledge of, and interest in, Africa, something which would have a great impact on my future.

A certain Dr. Joe Church was one of several medical missionaries who came from Emmanuel College. His son Mike was two years ahead of me. God used Dr. Joe in remarkable ways at the start of the Rwandan revival, despite numerous difficulties and mistakes he made as a new young doctor at Gahini, Rwanda, in the late 30s. It was a privilege to listen to this gracious man share something of his story when he visited the College.

Financially I had it much easier than today's students. Once into university I automatically qualified for a government grant covering full fees, board and lodging although it was subject to a means test. In other words, my father had to disclose his salary and assets and be required to pay a proportion of my grant accordingly. I never knew how much (if any) he paid, and how much the government chipped in, but it easily covered my needs. I came from that frugal post war era when one was very careful with finance, and my grant more than met my needs, particularly since I did not smoke or drink. John the Baptist and I had the same financial philosophy: "Be content with your wages" (Luke 3:14). I do not, in fact, have any recollection of any student who got into financial difficulties.

We had just three terms of eight weeks each at Cambridge, meaning we had a long summer holiday. There was much talk about what one might do during the "Long Vac" (the long vacation). I chose to take the basics of my degree in two years, meaning that I had to do the "Long Vac" term in the middle of my first summer holiday. I made some money picking strawberries just before that—a back breaking job in which we could not even enjoy the fruit of our labour because it had to be picked just before it was ripe so it would have a long shelf life. As pay was based on the amount picked we worked as fast as we could. The backache started half an hour after the start of work and continued all day.

After the "Long Vac" term and before the winter term started I worked as a waiter in a hotel in Ilfracombe. The place had seen better days; it catered mostly to coach tour operators who had negotiated special reduced rates. We made it a point to offer non-coach tour guests better service.

These two work experiences in the grittier, wider world were eye-openers. I now understood why strawberry pickers collapsed on their beds in the evenings without showering or washing their bedsheets as often as they might have, while the loose morals of the hotel staff came as a surprise to this somewhat naïve student coming from a sheltered family.

Cambridge during the mid-summer term was idyllic. There were far fewer students in the lecture rooms, labs and dissecting room, which also made it easier to make friends. One of my best investments at that time was a fifth interest—35 pounds sterling—in a punt, a small shallow boat, for use on "the Cam". After my three years there the punt was in bad shape, and I do not recall recouping our investment. However, the three years of pleasure it gave us were well worth the investment. There is little that compares to a lazy punt along the 'backs' at Cambridge on a sunny summer afternoon with an Addenbrook nurse aboard.

After my Hotel Ilfracombe experience I was delighted to return to Cambridge. I always travelled by train, sending my trunk PLA (passenger luggage in advance) for five shillings and sixpence! At the beginning of the semester there would be a huge pile of trunks stacked at the porters' lodge of the college; first you'd find your trunk, then you'd have to find someone to help carry it to your room. The very first time I sent my trunk that way it arrived damaged and with things missing. My father was convinced that someone working for the railways had broken into it. That was my first—but by no means last—confrontation with corruption.

I have always enjoyed travel, and after my second year at Emmanuel College planned a major expedition. On the 15th June, 1963, six of us Cambridge students set off in a VW bus. During the next thirteen weeks we drove 8,100 miles (over 13,000 km). We crossed Europe, Turkey, Syria, Lebanon, Jordan and Israel, and returned via Greece. Just prior to our arrival there had been riots in Turkey, and martial law was in force when we passed through. Disturbances in Syria and elections in Jordan did not affect us either.

Scripture Gift Mission had given us some Bible verses in various languages to distribute on the way. In Sofia, the capital of still-very-communist Bulgaria no one would take a copy. As we sped through a particular town the next day, however, a tract flew out a window and we saw people running into the street to see what we had dropped. From then on we regularly scattered leaflets from the window.

The daunting Bulgaria-Turkish border consisted of an "iron curtain" in the most literal sense of the word: a six foot high massive barbed wire fence with wooden observation towers in which guards peered through binoculars into Turkey. Bulgarian customs officials went through our two suitcases with a fine-toothed comb, yet failed to notice a bundle of tracts under one seat; we learned later that a group passing through soon after us were charged with distributing illegal literature, and were only released after a lengthy interrogation.

We drove towards Istanbul and crossed the Bosphorus from Europe into Asia. From there we drove south-eastward towards Syria and Lebanon where, much to my amazement, I learned that there were only some two hundred of the famed "cedars of Lebanon" left standing. Someone was drying some of this cedar wood in a nearby church, filling the sanctuary with a fabulous aroma. From there we tried to cross the mountains. Somewhere above the snowline our bus conked out; we had mismanaged our fuel reserves and were forced to push it uphill. Thankfully, however, the engine eventually kicked into gear and, using up the last drops of the fuel, made it to the snowy top. From the top of the pass we coasted into the Beka valley and Baalbeck, where we refueled.

A few days later we were crossing the Syrian desert to the amazing Roman remains at the oasis in Palmyra. At Petra, in arid but mountainous southern Jordan, we hiked to a massive monastery, one of the largest buildings ever carved out of solid rock. When we got there we bought the entire overpriced stock of drinks from an Arab vendor, though some of us thought we could defeat the battle with thirst by drinking from a small stream. I suffered from severe vomiting and diarrhea the next day.

Jerusalem was the high point of that trip. Before 1967 it was still a divided city. The left side of our Palestinian produced map was blank and labeled "Enemy occupied territory." We spent most of our time in East Jerusalem, in the old walled city still controlled by Jordan. We crossed into Israel through the unmarked Mandelbaum gate after negotiating concrete barriers, no-mans land and unoccupied houses. The Israeli frontier post welcomed us warmly. Unlike the old city we had just left, the 'New Jerusalem' felt much more European.

Political constraints prevented us from returning the way we came, so we had the bus loaded onto a ship, the T.S.S. Hermes, travelled "deck class" from Haifa to Athens, and drove back to England. The entire trip cost me a mere 60 pounds sterling.

My third year at Cambridge was dedicated to obtaining a degree in pathology. Delving into the depths of immunology and parasitology fascinated me.

My time at Cambridge was drawing to a close. I spent my last "long vacation" as a camp counselor at a YMCA camp in New York. My parents saw me off on this, my first of many trips across the North Atlantic. Most planes manage to take off half-way down the runway; our overloaded Boeing 707 Aer Lingus Student Charter needed the entire length before staggering skyward.

Camp McAllister was a lesson in race relations, though it took me some time to appreciate this. I was so busy adapting to the new culture that I did not sense any tensions below the surface. The camp "commandant" was white and the "adjutant" black. The campers consisted of an equal mixture of blacks and whites from the poorer districts of New York. Race relationships seemed easy and harmonious to me–until a particular section head had to be dismissed. In any case, I took over from the dismissed leader and the camp finished without further incident.

I was invited to speak at Sunday morning chapel twice. My subject was about forgiveness, something which suddenly seemed to me to be a very necessary ingredient to maintain harmony.

Because I was in the USA I missed my graduation ceremony from Cambridge. However, I received my Bachelor of Arts at a supplementary ceremony in September of that year. We proceeded five abreast from College in dinner jackets (tuxedos) white bow ties, tabs, a black gown and white fur-trimmed hoods through town to the senate house. In there we advanced five at a time to where the vice chancellor was sitting and, while each one of us held on to one of his fingers he said a few words of Latin over us. The written copy of my degree proved to be a very simple, easy-to-counterfeit, black and white affair with my name written on it with an ordinary typewriter! Those three undergraduate years at Cambridge were some of the most enjoyable of my life, though that was not true for everyone there.

During my second year, notices saying, "HAVE YOU BEEN CONVERTED?" were posted all over town. Cambridge was the first town in England to be converted from coal-gas to North Sea natural gas. One of the principal reasons why the town was at the top of the list was because of the high frequency of suicide by putting one's head in a coal-gas oven. Natural gas, on the other hand, does not contain any carbon monoxide and is therefore non-toxic. I had contact with one student who attempted suicide by slashing his wrists. I took it to be a plea for help rather than a real attempt to end his life, and trust I was able to help him a little.

Back then the final years of a medical education were not available at Cambridge, so several of us went to do three years of "clinical studies" at St Bartholomew's hospital in London, after which we would sit our final exams in Cambridge and be granted a second Cambridge degree.

Most teaching at 'Barts' took place around the beds of our patients, and I have been very grateful for this hands-on education. We were assigned a number of patients we had to follow as they went through various procedures, and we needed to be able to give a detailed answer to any question asked by the "prof" during the next ward round.

Two significant events took place towards the end of my medical education. Firstly, I spent three months in Montreal, a subject to which I will return in the next chapter. Secondly, I was awarded the top prize–the Brackenbury Scholarship–in surgery at Barts immediately before my final exams. I was shocked to receive this prize and, I suspect it was a surprise to my fellow students as well! As a result I could choose almost all my placements for the next four years of surgical training.

At the end of that period I sat the exams set by the Royal College of Surgeons of England, to be recognized as a general surgeon. It consisted of three parts with an extensive oral at the end. Only about 10% of examinees pass it. I'm not sure what I would have done if I had failed since I had arranged a research post in Toronto, Canada, to start a couple of weeks after the exams.

The main subject of conversation as we ended our training pertained to getting a top specialist position as quickly as possible. This normally meant medical work in London in a prestigious hospital. The idea of a general practice in the suburbs was definitely not on the agenda, and when I shared that I might go to Africa to practice surgery there, well, that was incomprehensible and disappointing to both classmates and family members.

Where did this idea of service in Africa come from? While at Cambridge, a talk Dr. Bill Capper gave at an Inter Varsity (Christian) Fellowship national conference on the first four verses of Luke's gospel greatly encouraged me. Unlike the subsequent hit-and-miss of medicine during the "dark ages", Bill explained that Luke's education followed the tradition of Hippocrates, the father of modern medicine. Luke was trained in a thoroughly scientific manner. Taught to observe carefully, then make a guess about causation, that is, to form a hypothesis, then to further test, observe, refine and confirm his guess. When researching his gospel he followed this procedure: he first acknowledged the work of others: "many have taken in hand to set forth in order, a declaration of those things which are most surely believed among us" (Luke 1:1). Then he described his methods as "delivered unto us, by those which from the beginning were eyewitnesses, and ministers of the word" (Luke 1:2). His results: "having followed all things closely for some time past" (Luke 1:3). His objective: "to write an orderly account....that you might know the truth concerning the things of which you have been informed" (Luke 1:3-4).

Excursion 1: Dr. Luke and the Evidence

Dr. Luke wanted us to wholeheartedly trust his information, so took great care to be precise in his descriptions. In my mind's eye I can see him making notes on papyrus about his patients. Now, however, he jots down notes of things that eyewitnesses heard Jesus say. He feared that legends would build up around this amazing individual, Jesus of Nazareth. He, however, wanted the facts, and tells how he delved into them. He does not want us to adopt a 'blind' faith, but one that is based on history, on what actually happened, on the history of God's interaction with man, and particularly through the person of Jesus Christ.

Luke's education is evident from his excellent Greek, as well as from the particular events he chooses to record. He is the one who shares the details of Mary's pregnancy and delivery; one can imagine him taking detailed notes as he interviewed Mary. He undoubtedly had many women patients; one finds an amazing tenderness to women throughout his gospel.

Dr. Capper pointed out the special medical terminology in the gospel of Luke and the Acts of the Apostles, which Luke also wrote. In Acts 3:7 he uses a medical term to describe the ankle bones of the cripple that Peter healed at the beautiful gate of the temple. In Acts 28:6 he used a word for an inflammatory oedema after Paul had been bitten by a snake.

Luke was a Gentile, the only non-Jewish writer of the whole Bible, and so he assumes nothing. You don't need to know your Old Testament to benefit from his accounts. He simply states the facts, and lets them speak for themselves. He emphasizes that he is writing to everyone by tracing Jesus' genealogy back to Adam. He addresses his works to a certain Theophilus, which also means "lover of God". Though Theophilus may have been a real person, he addressed all who are, at the very least, sympathetic towards the things of God. Today his carefully crafted and painstakingly researched biographies of Christ and Paul provide us with continuous historical links between Christ, His apostles, and the early church.

For the majority of students at Cambridge University, Bible teaching was not the way one spent Saturday evenings. It may be that my own lifelong crusade against being governed by cultural norms started then.

In any case, Jesus never promised popularity. Luke's version of Jesus' Sermon on the Mount turns the normal world-view upside down: "Blessed are you when men hate you, and when they exclude you and revile you, and cast out your name as evil, on account of the Son of man!" (Luke 6:22). I did not seek unpopularity but recognized that it might come "on account of the Son of man"; I realized I had to face the consequences of earnestly seeking God's will for my life.

Luke, it appeared, had chosen to relinquish his lucrative medical profession and hazard his well-being to be Paul's missionary companion. While each of the four gospel writers presented a biography of Jesus' life, they each had different ideas about what to include and what to leave out. Their choices were dictated in part by the audience for whom they were writing, in part by personal interest, and in part by their individual inspiration from the Holy Spirit. Luke concentrated on practical encouragements to faith. He also gave due attention to prayer.

One of his major themes—judging by the amount of space given to it—was money. He recorded more teaching on money than on any other subject. Of the thirty-nine parables of Jesus contained in Luke, sixteen refer to money. Only one of Jesus' parables about money found in the other three gospels was not included by him, notably the parable of the hidden treasure. The three parables that begin with "there was a rich man" are found only in his Gospel.

It has been said that there are two ways to be rich: to have all the money you could ever want, or to be satisfied with what you have. I have rarely had enough money to go far beyond my basic needs, but I praise God that He has kept me satisfied. I thank Him for all the little things and am amazed that when we needed bigger things (a house, a car, school fees), these were provided as well, as you will see in the coming chapters.

2

Bulstrode Manor, Gerrards Cross, Near London

ONE MINOR complication of studying at Barts Hospital was that their pediatric department was very small and very specialized; one could not get much idea of the breadth of children's illness among the mere forty or so beds there. I decided to look for a busier place in which to study the subject. A previous student had had a great time in Montreal Canada, so I applied to and was accepted for a three month exchange at Montreal Children's Hospital.

I also learned of the existence of a so-called "Gladstone Scholarship". After being interviewed by a committee of important liberals (which included the well-known historian and educator Alan Bullock) at the huge and somewhat intimidating Victorian headquarters of the UK Liberal party, they awarded me a scholarship. It paid for my trip to Canada.

I thoroughly enjoyed the bustle of down-town Montreal, "Mount Royal" park and, of course, ice hockey. The Forum, where the "Canadiens" played faced the hospital. I could get a ticket to stand at one end of the arena for just a dollar. At the same time the hospital gave me a wealth of experience in pediatrics.

After my stint in Montreal I purchased a Greyhound bus ticket ($99 for 99 days) in order to make my way to Texas, where my older sister was living. My travels took me through Toronto, where I knew of three Canadian medical students who had registered for the First International Conference of Christian Medical Students. I was on the organizing committee of this conference, to be held at Oxford University in July

1966, a month after my planned return to England. The purpose of the conference was to interest medical students from around the world in some of the difficult ethical issues they were likely to encounter in their future medical practices, as well as to encourage them in their Christian lives. The pressures of life as a junior doctor can shipwreck one's faith unless it is carefully nurtured. We had invited Dr. John Stott to give a series of Bible studies from the gospel of John.

While staying at the Central YMCA in Toronto I phoned the first of the three registrants on my list, a certain Nancy Houser. Her mother picked up the phone and she heard the voice of a "mature" individual who would receive her offspring at Oxford. She had expressed concern that her 21 year old daughter thought of traveling to England in the company of two male medical students.

"Come round to dinner and I will invite the other two to come as well," she suggested. She told me later that when she saw me standing at the door she thought, "why, he's only a boy..."

After the Oxford conference Nancy and I started corresponding. I saw her again two years later in London, when she was en route to Africa. She had taken the speaker at a Christian Medical and Dental Society (CMDS) conference in Toronto, a Dr. Don Gibson, at his word: Don had stated that medical personnel of any type were badly needed in Africa. When Nancy, a 1st year medical student at the time had asked him how she could be used, he was initially taken aback, but then arranged for her to help in the laboratory of Mengo Hospital, in Kampala, Uganda. The CMDS agreed to pay her airfare and Mengo Hospital agreed to provide board and lodging in exchange for her work in their laboratory. Since she was going to Uganda anyway, the Canadian directors of Africa Inland Mission, old family friends, urged her to visit the Congo, their former field of service, as well. "We will help you get a visa. When you get there just say Peter and Mary-Lou sent you!"

Nancy took them at their word as well. She made the grueling 16 hour trip from Kampala to Congo straddling the gear shift of a land rover driven by a missionary called Jean Shramm. They planned to travel through to a place called Rethy, just across the Congolese border, and then travel down to Nyankunde, close to the southern end of Lake Albert. Congo was just recovering from the Simba rebellion and there were no road signs (there still are not many today). The roads were in a dismal state, just narrow tracks through the bush. Whenever they came to a Y

23

junction after dark they would pray, and take turns guessing which road to take. They arrived safe and sound!

A cooperative effort by 5 different mission agencies had enabled a certain Dr. Carl Becker to re-establish a hospital at Nyankunde. Dr. Becker had returned to the Congo two years earlier, at the end of the Simba Rebellion, during which much of the medical infrastructure in the country had been destroyed. He had recruited Dr. Helen Roseveare from Nebobongo Hospital to found a good quality nurses' training school, to train students from all over the north-east of Congo.

What impressed Nancy most during her week at the Nyankunde school was the standard of medical care and the intensive medical and spiritual formation being given to young Congolese men who would otherwise be unemployed. By the end of that visit she had decided to return there for her elective two years later. She had no funds, and her family had told her they would not be able to help her beyond her undergraduate degree, but Nancy was convinced that God wanted her to return to the Congo, and that He would work things out. And, indeed, she received a travel scholarship from Smith Kline and French, which enabled her to spend 2 months in 1970 with Dr. Helen at the Nyankunde nursing school. On each of her African trips I intercepted Nancy as she travelled through London.

My life took a radical change on a blustery day in September 1970. Nancy had completed her second stint in the Congo and was en route back to Canada. I took her on a date to the Royal Festival Hall, a panoramic restaurant overlooking the Thames which had become a favorite of mine while working towards a Fellowship in Surgery from the Royal College of Surgeons in London.

After relating some of her experience in Congo, Nancy shared that she sensed God calling her to work long term at Nyankunde—and that she felt this strong enough that if need be she would go as a single. By this time I knew enough of Nancy's determination and discipline to realize that if she said she was going, then she would! What was a man to do...?

"We can go together," I said. There comes a point when you realize what and who really matters and always will, and what and who never really did—and, more importantly, how radical the choices one faces if one is serious about following Jesus for life.

I had been interested in mission work for a long time. I was in awe of

Dr. Joe Church, an alumni of my alma mater, Emmanuel College Cambridge, whom God had used in the Rwanda revival. I had led a prayer group that interceded for the Sudan, and my church had made me their representative for the Leprosy Mission. When Nancy shared about God's call to serve at Nyankunde in the Democratic Republic of Congo, I became equally sure that God was calling me to go with her. There were no blinding lights, no thunderous roars—just the assurance that this was where God wanted us to serve Him.

I can appreciate that my peers thought me foolish for turning my back on the life and luxury of a well paid surgeon. I have no regrets. For the last 40 plus years, my life has been an exciting journey. Not only have I done a lot of interesting surgery, albeit in the most primitive conditions, I have had the privilege of training many medical workers in Congo. And time and again I have been amazed at God's wonderful provisions. I have been "satisfied with good things" (Luke 1:53). The skeptic may say that it is all the result of careful planning, wild coincidences or the luck of the draw; for Nancy and me, ours has been a life of trust and faith in Him. Faith: Forsaking All I Trust Him.

The next decision we faced pertained to the type of organization we might go with. We could have applied to an international body like the World Health Organization, but feared we would get bogged down in politics rather than hands-on medicine. We could have gone with a government-sponsored organization, but these can be corrupt and disorganized.

Church-sponsored organizations provide a significant portion of medical care offered in Sub-Saharan Africa, as they have both the ethical base and the discipline needed to offer a worthwhile service. In the end the question was reduced to two choices: should we join one of the five mission agencies that worked at Nyankunde or would we go independently?

All missionaries tend to be strong willed—they have to be, or they would not persevere in the difficult and often dangerous places where the good news of God's grace in Jesus Christ has not yet been heard. "Independent" missionaries, however, can be particularly individualistic. We chose to join a larger team in order to profit from all a good mission organization can provide: encouragement, advice, orientation, a channel for finance from supporting churches, and the connection with a church group in Africa. Either way, as independents or with a mission we would have to be supported by our respective churches and a few individuals.

Five different agencies worked at Nyankunde. Nancy had had close contact with one of them in Canada, and I with another in UK. We visited both of them in their UK offices on the same day. The morning appointment was in Finsbury Park, London. We arrived by subway train at a station that had not yet been rebuilt after being bombed in the war. The mission was on the third floor of a row house. We climbed the uncarpeted stairs to the CEO's office. He had to turn up his hearing aid to hear our story, and then spelled out the conditions we would need to meet before we could join his mission.

That afternoon's meeting was in Gerrards Cross, outside London. The weather was glorious. We made our way from the train station to a marvelous Victorian manor built by the 12th Duke of Somerset in 1865. The British director of Worldwide Evangelization for Christ (WEC International) suggested we go outside and sit by one of the ornamental lakes. After hearing our story he expressed his excitement at the fact that God was leading us to Nyankunde. He shared that WEC's role was to help people like us to fulfill God's calling on their lives. If WEC could help us, and if we agreed to the "Principles and Practice" of the mission, we would be warmly welcomed into their ranks.

WEC is a "faith" mission. This derogatory term was first coined by the press in the mid 19th century to describe the way George Muller ran the orphanages he had founded in Bristol. An ordinary man with an implicit trust in an extraordinary God, Muller took the Bible's promises about God supplying all one needs when doing His will at face value. As a result he never asked anyone but God for the necessary finances to run his ministry—even going so far as to refuse to answer if someone asked him point blank what his needs were. He was convinced that if he made his needs known to God, God would prompt the right people without recourse to human solicitation.

Of course all those who count themselves as Christ's disciples are to trust God to supply their needs, regardless of the size of their income or the sum of their assets. Living by faith is much more than trusting God to meet financial needs. It implies trusting Him to provide for all of one's requirements, be they temporal, physical, mental or spiritual. However, WEC International is one of those "faith missions" which encourage their members to look to the Lord rather than to human institutions to meet their financial needs. In practice this means that its members may not ask for financial support from anyone other than God. They are free to give reports on their work, but not in such a way as to actively solicit funds.[1]

One major thrust of both Jesus Christ's formal and informal instructions to His twelve disciples pertained to teaching them to trust Him in increasing measure. Instead of being engulfed by anxiety, fear and doubt, He wanted them to look to Him at all times: when the wine ran out at a wedding, during a storm at sea, or when their world fell apart during his arrest and false conviction.

Surely the Christian can trust God to supply everything he or she needs if his life and ministry follows His direction! Of course this does not preclude seeking prayer support, nor does it preclude sharing honestly and regularly about both the successes and failures of our ministry. Churches and supporters have a right to know how their representatives overseas use the funds they so sacrificially give.

Nancy and I married in 1972; our wedding was both a celebration and a farewell. "What's this I hear about you going abroad?" a prominent Toronto accountant asked at the wedding. "If you both work full time in Canada for five years without starting a family, and let me invest your money, you'll be financially independent for life. Then go to Africa..." We turned down his advice. We were young and perhaps naïve, but keen to test dependence on God.

We left for Africa two weeks after our marriage—and have never regretted that decision. In fact, we left in style! Nancy's parents gamely drove us to New York, where we boarded the cruise ship the Queen Elizabeth II. I remember looking at the Statue of Liberty with Nancy as we slipped away from Manhattan Island and into the Atlantic. The five day journey across the Atlantic was wonderful. There were lectures, concerts and shows, interspersed with walks around the ship, fine dining, and other activities that people get up to on their honeymoon. The food was excellent; we never ordered the same thing, so we could savour it all.

One of the advantages of travelling on the Q.E. II was that we could take as much baggage as we wanted, including a huge trunk we anticipated shipping straight to Africa from Europe. However our first

---

[1] Note: the organization is allowed to respond positively to invitations by foundations or other charities for available funds for capital development projects.

stop was Antwerp where we spent five months learning tropical medicine in French.

We had both applied for scholarships to pay for this course, I through the British Council and Nancy through the Canadian Council. Nancy was informed that she had been awarded her bursary, but I received a letter saying I had been refused. We thought we could get by on the one scholarship. The official administering the funds in Brussels quickly verified Nancy's credentials.

"What about you?" he asked me.

"I was informed that I had been refused."

"I will check." When the man returned he informed us that another British person had cancelled his application, and that I could have the scholarship in his stead!

We made our way to the International Student Centre in Antwerp, where someone recommended an apartment for rent. It was large—but only had a single cold water tap in the kitchen, while the upstairs shower, shared with another renter, gave a trickle of warm water if you turned the flow way down: you could have a good shower in cold water or a pathetic one under a warm dribble. The bedroom was unheated, but with a large skylight. A hot water bottle, a pile of 5 blankets and cuddling close did the trick.

Our course on medical orientation to Africa at the 'Institut de Medecine Tropicale' was taught by a number of doctors who had left Congo in 1960 at independence. Their attitude to the country was not necessarily positive, but five months later we had covered the full gamut of tropical medicine. I wondered how I would pass the exams as my French was barely passable; Nancy's was much better. We spent most evenings deciphering a large quantity of copied notes. We also took a remedial French course, and had supper at the International Students Centre, where we tried to practice our language on the other students.

Our scholarship money was paid through the Post Office, which operated only in Flemish. Unable to figure out which services were offered at which wicket, we would finally arrive at the head of a long queue, only to be told we needed to join another one and wait a further half hour. One month they gave us a 10,000 franc note. Although they themselves would not accept notes higher than 1,000 francs, they refused to give us anything smaller. Fortunately our landlord, a shopkeeper, agreed to change it for us.

As a U.K citizen I did not need a visa for Belgium but Nancy did. As instructed by the Belgian embassy in Canada, we duly went to the local police station in Antwerp. After half an hour or so a policeman finally waved us over. Using one finger on an ancient typewriter he eventually produced six copies of our residence permits; one for each of Belgium's districts. Halfway through he asked us for six photos. "Sorry we only have three."

"Well give me those." A week later we received a letter: "Please present yourself at the police station with your passport at noon...". We were there at noon. The policeman on duty took Nancy's passport, after which we waited for the requisite half hour. "Where are the three missing photographs?"

"Sir, the letter asked for a passport but didn't mention photographs." A week later we received another letter asking us to report to the police station. This time we had our three photos, along with a picnic lunch for the inevitable thirty minute wait. "Here are the three photographs, sir."

"No need. The letter only asks for a passport," came the reply. We handed over the requisite document, went to the waiting room, and had lunch. Thirty minutes later the officer reappeared, to ask rather sheepishly for the three remaining photographs. We returned on the fourth week—with our lunches—to pick up the visa. If the colonial power operated like this, little wonder the bureaucracy of the Democratic Republic of Congo turned out the way it is...

Although the tropical medicine course was essential for our future practice of medicine in Congo, it was disappointing in that it did not involve any real, live patients—even though the institute was connected to a hospital for tropical diseases. Sometimes teachers simply read the duplicated notes they had given us. Once again, the long shadow of the colonial past can be seen in the present day study of medicine in the Congo, where courses are often very theoretical but with little practical experience to offer.

We were able to purchase a small green van, with which we travelled to Amsterdam, Paris, Oldenberg and many places within Belgium, including weekend visits to Liege, to see the family of Dr. Marianne Charlier, whom we had met in Toronto at the Second International Conference of Christian Medical Students, two weeks prior to our wedding. The visits to Liege mattered, because Mrs. Charlier never hesitated to correct my French. Up to that point I had no idea one could

29

make so many mistakes in a single sentence.

We both managed to pass the final exams and receive our diplomas in Tropical Medicine and Hygiene. We drove our van to the United Kingdom, to the WEC headquarters at Gerrards Cross, for four months of missionary orientation. This was when the organization gets to know you, and you it. Besides orientation lectures and participation in various ministries, we "missionary candidates" also helped maintain the huge mansion with its acres of gardens.

Although our disposable income was very small compared to that of our wealthy colleagues, "Bulstrode", as the WEC mansion was known locally, was only the first of several large, beautiful houses we have had the privilege of living in. Years later we would move into the largest house on one of the most prestigious streets in Hamilton, Canada, surrounded by rich Jewish doctors in much smaller houses working long hours to maintain their standard of living. And during the intervening years friends often let us use their beautiful homes for short periods of time when we have passed through the UK or Canada.

While at "Bulstrode" we tried to save every penny for our airfare and start-up costs in Africa. One morning someone mentioned during morning prayers that the fund used to cover the mission's general expenses was dangerously low. The speaker, a man called David Batchelor, then mentioned that he had just received a significant gift which he had not yet tithed and said he felt led to put a tenth of this gift into the general fund. Then he quoted from Malachi, "Bring your tithes into the storehouse and see if I won't open the windows of heaven to give a blessing", and challenged the rest of us: "Is there anybody else here who has received a gift and hasn't tithed it yet? Maybe you should consider giving it to the general fund."

Nancy and I realized that we had not tithed all that we had received, and later that morning wrote out a cheque which I took to the finance office. At three o'clock that same afternoon, I was told to report to the reception area, where the treasurer of my home church in Guildford, a personal friend, was waiting for me. "We received a significant gift for you in Sunday's collection," Falkner Hole said. "I was not sure I should trust such a large gift to the post, so I brought it round in person." The amount was several times larger than that which we had given to the mission that very morning. The event seemed to us a dramatic example of Jesus' words, "Give and it will be given to you; a good measure, pressed down, shaken together and running over, will be poured into your lap. For with the measure you use, it will be measured to you" (Luke 6:38).

Excursion 2: The "Life of Faith"

In the early part of the 20th century there was a lot of discussion in evangelical Christian circles about "living by faith", that is, living in an attitude of complete trust in the fact that God, who knows our needs, would also supply all that we, his children, need. And there are, indeed, many Bible passages that would support this idea. For instance, Luke records Jesus as saying: "Therefore I tell you, do not be anxious about your life, what you shall eat, nor about your body, what you shall put on. For life is more than food, and the body more than clothing. Consider the ravens: they neither sow nor reap, they have neither storehouse nor barn, and yet God feeds them. Of how much more value are you than the birds!" (Luke 12:23-24).

Faith is assurance, confidence, reliance on the fact that whatever God has stated in the Bible is true, and that He will act according to what He has said. George Muller testified toward the end of his life that,

"When I first began to allow God to deal with me, relying on Him, taking Him at His word, and set out fifty years ago simply relying on Him for myself, family, taxes, traveling expenses and every other need, I rested on the simple promises I found in the sixth chapter of Matthew. I believed the Word, I rested on it and practiced it. I took God at His Word... I began in a little way. At first, I was able to trust the Lord for ten dollars, then for a hundred dollars, then for a thousand dollars, and now, with the greatest ease, I could trust Him for a million dollars, if there was occasion. But first, I should quietly, carefully, deliberately examine and see whether what I was trusting for, was something in accordance with His promises in His written Word."[2]

The Bible encourages us to ask for whatever it is we need. Who should we ask from? Clearly from the one we believe is able to meet the need. For someone who is "living by faith in God" that person is God himself. If you are going to look to Him to supply your needs you must

---

[2] Muller, G 1861. *The Life of Trust*, Boston: Gould and Lincoln.

ask Him. You should pray.

The faith missions were called that by the general public because they appeared to actually practice this to such an extent that Hudson Taylor, the founder of the China Inland Mission (OMF today), could say "God's work done in His way will never lack His support". There are still a number of Christian organizations that call themselves "Faith Ministries" because they genuinely believe that God will supply their needs. They tend not to be attached to any particular denomination, which tend to support their own organizations financially.

In fact, the way the different "faith ministries" apply their "faith principles" can vary considerably. The first variant was followed by George Muller, who would never tell anyone exactly how much money he needed. He believed that if money was to come from a particular person God alone would put it on someone's heart to give.

Secondly, there are those "faith missions" which boldly announce their needs, and expect the Lord to supply their needs through interested believers. In other words, they have no qualms about firmly encouraging Christians to give to them. They will often fix the sum of money that a particular missionary candidate will need and will not allow the individual to fulfill the call of God before they can testify that *they* (my emphasis) have raised the sum required. Generally help is given in this fund raising process, with suggestions being given as to what proportion a home church should contribute or who is most likely to pony up.

Thirdly, there are the "faith missions" which will publicize their needs but not directly solicit for funds. They expect God to lay their needs on the hearts of particular individuals or churches who will then know how and to whom they should give. A variant of the latter are the organizations that will only allow their members to mention specific needs to people who specifically ask to know about them.

Lastly, Henry Nouwen, in his book *A Spirituality of Fundraising* adopts a middle position which sounds, to me, great in theory but difficult to put into practice. "If our security is totally in God, then we are free to ask for money," he states, and goes on to explain that "once we are prayerfully committed to placing our *whole* (my emphasis) trust in God and have become clear that we are concerned *only* (my emphasis) for the kingdom; once we have learned to love the rich for who they are rather than what they have; and once we believe that we have something of great value to give them, then we will have no trouble at all in asking someone for a large sum of money."[3] Nouwen presents a number of conditions to be met before one can ask for funds. Being who he was, he could no doubt fulfill these conditions; I fear that I might ask for support simply for my own comfort, rather than only for the kingdom.

The Old Testament taught God's people to tithe. The young man of Luke 18:12, for instance, was quick to point out that "I fast twice in the week, I give tithes of all that I possess." Through the discipline of tithing God sought to instill in His Old Covenant people the concept of giving. One tenth of all a person's income, including all of his or her animals and farm produce, was to be given to God (Numbers 18:26). In fact, the English word "tithe" is derived from the Old English for a tenth. God challenged His people to test Him in this matter. "Bring the whole tithe into the storehouse... Test me in this,' says the Lord Almighty, 'and see if I will not throw open the flood-gates of heaven and pour out so much blessing that you will not have room enough for it" (Malachi 3:10).

There was one occasion in the Old Testament where asking a human agency rather than (or even as well as) asking God was considered wrong. Ezra and his company had been given a considerable amount of money which they were to carry across the desert from Babylon to Jerusalem, an area where there was considerable danger from thieves and robbers. "I was ashamed to ask the king for a band of soldiers and horsemen to help us against the enemy in the way: because we had spoken unto the king, saying, The hand of our God is upon all them for good that seek him; but his power and his wrath is against all them that forsake him" (Ezra 8:22). Ezra was ashamed to ask for help from the king since he had boldly stated that he would get all the help he needed from God.

The New Testament does not give a lot of teaching about giving to church work. Whereas the Old Testament taught that one tenth of one's "first fruits" (i.e. gross income) should be tithed (Lev. 23:10), the New Testament—particularly Luke's gospel—emphasises complete, 100%, giving of all we possess for the kingdom: "Sell all that you have and distribute to the poor" Jesus told the rich young ruler (Luke 18:22). To the crowd around him he stated that "if any man will come after me, let him deny himself, and take up his cross daily, and follow me" (Luke 9:23).

---

[3] Nouwen, H 2010. *A Spirituality of Fundraising*. Nashville: Upper Room Books.

What was the response? The disciples pulled their ships ashore, forsook all, and followed him (Luke 5:11). Then, as they were walking along, they saw a tax collector named Levi sitting in the tax office, "and Jesus said to him, 'Follow me'. And he left everything, and rose and followed him" (Luke 5:27-28).

The phrase "the life of faith" does not actually occur anywhere in the Bible. It does, however, accurately describe the attitude the disciples exhibited as they "forsook all and followed Jesus". Forsaking, leaving, faith and trust (in God) are all attitudes that Luke records Jesus as encouraging us to adopt. Although it is easy for me to testify about the reliability of these divine promptings now, it took me years to discover that God really will provide.

The idea of the "missionary call" has fallen out of vogue. Today the preferred term is "one's vocation", i.e. doing a job not just for financial rewards but because it is interesting, satisfying and worthwhile, something which uses our talents, abilities, experience and education. We'd like our "vocation" to be stretching, but not too much so... When Jesus "called" his disciples it was not just to a vocation but to forsake all or, put another way, to put everything they had on the line. In Luke 5:11 two poor fishermen named James and John "left everything and followed him (Jesus)." They left their boats, their careers and their livelihood on the shore of the lake of Galilee in order to join Jesus' nomadic missionary life. They must have left wives and possibly children and other relatives behind for long periods of time. In Luke 5:28 we find Levi (also known as Matthew), a rich tax collector, doing the same thing. He completely abandoned his office and everything connected with it.

The financial advisor at our wedding encouraged us to work towards financial independence; Jesus encourages the exact opposite: complete dependence upon Himself as opposed to any man made financial system.

Financial independence is the aim of many, and it is calculated according to the abundance of a person's possessions (Luke 12:15). Judging from the size of the business sections of our newspapers many people spend inordinate amounts of time seeking to increase their investments—or at least seeking the safest place of refuge for their wealth. If, however, my present ongoing relationship with my creator God is meaningful to me at all then, it seems to me, that His priorities must play a large part in the way I spend money. If I believe that He is sovereign and omnipotent then I will realize that ultimately He is the source of my wealth, however big or small that may be, and that I should be spending it primarily on His purposes as opposed to my own.

I do not imagine that the average billionaire takes eternity into consideration when considering his next investment. According to Jesus, however, no matter how intelligent his investments, he is a fool if he did not factor in eternity (Luke 12:20-21).

Jesus taught His disciples to "travel light". He told them to go with "no money, no purse, and no bag" (Luke 10:4). The parallel passage in Matthew states that they go without gold, silver or copper (Matthew 6:8). And today Jesus continues to challenges us to resist collecting an abundance of earthly goods.

Instead of dwelling on the Old Testament command to tithe, Jesus exhorts His disciples to be generous to the point of pain. Luke continues to encourage us to be generous irrespective of the cost or the results: "Give to everyone who begs from you; and of him who takes away your goods do not ask for them again" (Luke 6:30). How much do we give? The principle is that with the measure that we give, we will receive (Luke 6:38). Rather than holding tightly to our money we are encouraged to do some good by spreading it around a little. J. Paul Getty is reported as saying, "Money is like manure; you have to spread it around or it smells".

3

Centre d'Accueil Protestant (CAP), Kinshasa, Congo

WE LEFT FOR the Congo two weeks after completing our missionary orientation with WEC International. Back in 1973 Kinshasa, the capital city of the Congo, was an interesting mix of the colonial and the post-colonial. We stayed at what had been the United Mission House, a marvelous colonial remnant with waiters serving in not-too-clean whitish uniforms with brass buttons. The uniforms were dispensed with soon afterwards, and the mission house had only recently changed its name to the Centre d'Accueil Protestant (CAP), French for "The Protestant Guest House". Across the road, on the Congo River and right in the heart of the city, was the Baptist guest house. The Baptists had been the first to open a missionary guest house in Kinshasa. Beside the CAP was LECO, a massive printing shop in the process of changing its name to CEDI. Their place was overrun with rats; the creatures liked the warmth emanating from the reservoirs of molten metal on the large monotype machines.

Up the road from CEDI was the large International Church of Kinshasa, a wooden building with gothic windows and pews which would not have looked out of place on the Canadian prairies. There was nothing else like it in the city. Services were in English, mainly for the expatriate missionary community.

During our first night under the threadbare blankets of the guest house I had a mild panic attack: although I had travelled extensively across North America, Europe, and Asia I had never done so with a wife, for whom I suddenly felt very responsible. I became very anxious. That night we talked about my feelings, then realized afresh that God was with us in this adventure. He would guide us, protect us and see us through! It was a question of trusting in the guidance we had received. I learned that the opposite of faith and trust is not doubt, but anxiety.

We had to spend six weeks in Kinshasa to get registered as medical practitioners. The rest of the WEC missionary team was stationed in the north-east of the country, some 2000 km away from us by river and some very poor roads. There were times during the first weeks when we felt very cut off, lonely and unsupported.

We spent a month at the Institut Médical Évangélique (IME), a large hospital in Kimpese run jointly by several mission groups. It was the model that Dr. Becker had used when he established the Centre Médical Évangélique (CME) in Nyankunde. Sadly, our orientation here was less than ideal. Nancy was put in charge of the pediatrics ward—where at least one baby died every night of malaria or sleeping sickness. After working at Toronto Sick Children's Hospital, where deaths were very rare, this took some getting used to. I did my first cesarean section here, also with no supervision. C sections had not been a part of my general surgical training. The patient was a young 17 year old who had been in obstructed labor for several days, and had only just been carried to the hospital. After the operation she developed tissue death where the baby's head had been pushing against the bones of her hips, and she died of infection about four days later. It was a very rude introduction to medicine and surgery in Congo, during which we received very little encouragement or supervision. Life in the guest house at Kimpese, however, was a great opportunity to meet and learn from both Congolese and expatriate missionaries, both long and short-termers.

The public health program at Kimpese was well organized, and we learned much as we travelled with the mobile team to encourage good health in outlying villages. Teaching sessions were done using brightly colored flip charts, and then mothers with their under 5's would line up to have their children weighed to see if they were developing normally. The weight was plotted graphically on a "road to health" chart. A drop in weight might signal a minor problem, like a cold, or a major problem such as bad nutrition. Children whose weight had dropped were directed to a "triage" nurse for further medical treatment and/or counseling. At the same time pregnant women were examined and, based mostly on their past medical history, a decision was made on whether they could have their baby in the village or if they should be encouraged to travel to

37

Kimpese for the delivery. Finally the team would try to spend time with the village elders in order to learn what the community's problems were, and inspect toilets and the water source.

After spending almost a month at Kimpese we returned to Kinshasa to complete our exposure to the Congolese public health system. The Congolese tried to maintain the system left by the Belgians, but due to underfunding and understaffing the results were not great. At times there was not even fuel for the public health vehicles. At a venereal disease clinic we visited prostitutes who were asked to come in every two months for a blood test for syphilis. Blood was drawn using large silver reusable needles; we now know that this was probably a major way in which AIDS was being transmitted.

After completion of this stage of our orientation we had to visit the Department of Public Health for an interview with the Director General, a Dr. Tshibuabua, after which we received our certificates to practice medicine in the Congo. We were running out of money, and happy to leave the expensive capital, when we received a message from the WEC team, up-country: "We would like you to stay in Kinshasa until you receive your permanent visas." Then, quite miraculously it seemed to us, we received the one and only note we ever received from the "Banque Commerciale Zairoise" to say that they had some money for us: how they found us in a city of, what was then, three million people, still amazes me. Our church in Canada, Little Trinity, had woken up to the fact that we were their missionaries, and sent the cash: just enough to help us complete the stay in Kinshasa, and join the WEC team on the other side of this vast country (the church has continued to support us faithfully ever since, for which we are very grateful.)

Knowing what we know now about Congolese banks, it amazes me even more that we received the money within half an hour. Not only is the Congo a bureaucratic nightmare, the banking system deteriorated to the point of collapse during our years there. Many times money sent to us ended up in someone else's account, or the bank would deny that it had arrived when, in fact, they were sitting on it. Eventually it became impossible to transfer money through the national banking system. Thankfully, there are small signs of improvement today among the multiplicity of banks that now operate in the country.

Fearing that the huge (the size of western Europe) and rich country might fracture into multiple smaller countries, the country's first prime-minister, Patrice Lumumba, made the administration in the capital as strong as possible. Getting our permanent visa in Kinshasa made sense, as you could not get it anywhere else. One side-effect of our extended stay in the capital was that we were inundated with requests for supplies by people living "up-country". When we finally headed for the airport we were, beside our own personal baggage, carrying a huge amount of other stuff, including two artificial legs and large quantities of medicines.

We had to fly from Kinshasa to Bunia some 2000km away; there is no road between the two cities, though one could do it by a combination of river and road. Kinshasa's Ndjili Airport is an unforgettable experience. For many years there was a single, one-way mirror at arrivals with a 3 inch slot under it. You slipped your passport through the slot and hoped you would be let into the country. Tucking a dollar bill into the document helped. I always felt silly and somewhat intimidated standing in front of that huge mirror knowing the fellow on the other side could see me clearly.

We were booked on a 36 seat Fokker Friendship plane to Bunia. It was 6 A.M. and inside the terminal chaos reigned. Huge crowds heading to various parts of the country were pushing and shoving with the help of family members around the single departures desk. It seemed that several flights were scheduled to leave at 6 in the morning. Luggage was transported above people's heads from the back. Our relief was boundless after we'd finally paid for our excess baggage, received a boarding pass and eventually boarded the turboprop. There were still two empty seats. We were the only two whites on the plane. Just as we started to relax we learned that 38 boarding passes had been issued. A message rang from the intercom. "Would Mr. and Mrs. Wood please leave the plane!" We refused at first: we had confirmed our booking months earlier! When a soldier came on board to inform us that our baggage was now on the tarmac and would disappear if we did not get off we caved in and got off.

It was 1973, and there was an anti-white bias in the country—partly as a result of President Mobutu's "Objectif 80". By 1980 Congo was supposed to be functioning so well that it would be able to dispense with further expatriate help. It certainly forced us to see how quickly we could train someone else to do our job. However, it also encouraged the Congolese to adopt an attitude of superiority, create discomfort for expatriates whenever they could, and exploit them as much as possible before they were forced to leave. They wanted to profit materially in the short term; not much thinking went into how they might profit from the educational input outsiders could provide. Thankfully, the anti-white bias changed over the years. We have been made to feel increasingly welcome, particularly after the 1994-2003 war, when there was a huge exodus of missionaries. Our African colleagues came to see that we are not there to make money; now they go out of their way to make sure we are well looked after.

It should be said that after forcing us off the plane, Air Zaire treated us well. They put us into a hotel for the night and gave us first class tickets to a place called Kisangani for the next day. Although we needed to pay extra for first class, our baggage allowance was larger, so we paid less in excess. First class consisted of the first three rows of seats.

There was no one to meet us in Kisangani, and we didn't know anyone there. However, I remembered reading about the Christian printing operation called LECO running a ministry there (later renamed CEDI), and found a taxi to take us there. What relief to be welcomed by Ed and Doreen! They got us on a small plane to Bunia a few days later where, to our amazement, Dr. Helen Roseveare was waiting to welcome us "home"! That dear woman had gone out to meet every plane arriving in Bunia for days in a row.

Excursion 3: Healthy relationships are the key to true wealth

Jesus said to his disciples, "I tell you, do not be anxious about your life, what you shall eat, nor about your body, what you shall put on. For life is more than food, and the body more than clothing. Consider the ravens: they neither sow nor reap, they have neither storehouse nor barn, and yet God feeds them. Of how much more value are you than the birds!" (Luke 12:22-26).

As mentioned earlier, the Bible describes the opposite of faith not as doubt but as anxiety. It calls us to trust God in all circumstances—and our level of trust can be gauged by our anxiety level. I had had awful feelings of unease and anxiety deep in my gut while in Kinshasa. Until the journey to Africa I had always felt in control, or had had 'props' to support me. In any case I'd only been responsible for myself, not also for a wife—who seemed to sleep much more calmly at night than I did! It is one thing to know the theory: our organization's formal declaration states that "God is our provider. We affirm our faith in Him to supply all our spiritual and material needs, believing that the following Scriptures entitle us to do so: Psalm 23:1; Matthew 6:33; 2 Corinthians 9:8; Philippians 4:10-20. We trust in God alone." The time had come to put theory into practice.

It took some time to get over that initial anxiety—and it has taken a lifetime of seeing God undertake to bring us to the point where we are both willing and comfortable to return to an area where there are at present some 44 rebel groups operating, and where armed robbery is only too common. Yes, God has protected through war and displacement in the past, but will He continue to do so in the future?

First of all, we are to pray to God, to cast all our cares on Him in the assurance that He cares about us (1 Peter 5:7). Next, we are responsible for communicating effectively with God's people; I am amazed at how much prayer our communications have generated, and have often been humbled when someone tells me that they pray for us on a daily basis.

We have been threatened but never injured. We have had difficult times financially (about which I will share later), but at other times we have been surprised at how God has provided seemingly miraculously. We have been amazed at how He has "satisfied us with good things" (Luke 1:53). We have never been without food or clothes.

"Take nothing with you" (Luke 9:3) is a call for faith in Christ—to trust him completely to provide for our needs. And He does do so! Maybe not all we want at times, but certainly all we need. For many years we lived in a country where there was little else but God in which one could place one's trust—and he has not disappointed us. We have been afraid, we have felt isolation, but never abandoned. And in the process we have come to be accepted into a wonderful family of Africans.

I once treated the son of a very wealthy London businessman. Much to the family's consternation, the boy had leukemia. His father instructed me to get the best medical care, medicines and treatment. Financial considerations were irrelevant. But all the money in the world could not buy the lad's health. As the child slipped away my heart went out to the father. The man was heartbroken, not just because he had lost his only son, but because he had been confronted with a problem he could not solve by throwing money at it. He was no longer in control. For the first time he encountered something that his money could not acquire: health for his son and heir.

Many people live under the delusion that money is the key to achieving control and happiness in their lives. "A little more money and I will control my happiness, my destiny." Satan, the great deceiver, must rub his hands in glee when he sees someone buy into this logic. The truth is that happiness is not found in money but in relationships. Healthy relationships, not possessions, are the key to true wealth. Who are you living with? Who are you working with? How are your family dynamics? What of your relationship with God? According to Jesus our relationships with others and God will determine how happy we will be. Happiness (blessedness) can be great in poverty if we feel accepted and surrounded by family in a "kingdom" (Luke 6:20).

Jesus called his disciples to follow him. He could see the shallowness of their lives and offered an alternative: "I've no place to lay my head – follow me!" he stated. "I have no abiding city in this world—follow me!" Put God first, others next, and yourself at the bottom. Fix your eyes on that which is ahead. Don't grasp the past. Forget what is past and press on!

This is the sense of Luke 9, where Jesus sent the disciples to preach the kingdom of God, and to heal. "Stay where you are offered hospitality," he counsels them, "wherever they do not receive you, when you leave that town shake off the dust from your feet as a testimony against them." We have been wonderfully received by the African church. In spite of corruption, warfare, extreme selfishness in the country and in spite our own many faults, we have developed numerous rich relationships. These have enriched us in ways the wealthy of this world can only dream about.

4

Centre Médical Évangélique, Nyankunde

UPON ARRIVAL in Nyankunde we were asked to take over the very well organized, accredited nursing training school established by Dr. Helen Roseveare. Before she left in 1973 the school's academic level was raised from auxiliary nursing to a nursing diploma level. As soon as Helen had moved out we moved into her little thatched house. She left us all her office supplies, furniture, her small car, her cook and a housekeeper who only spoke Swahili. We were rich!

Helen gave us five weeks of orientation, much of it teaching us basic Swahili. Although teaching and all hospital business was done in French the vast majority of patients knew only Swahili. Another aspect of our orientation was a 500 km truck trip Helen took us on to Ibambi and Nebobongo, the center of WEC's missionary work in Congo. Because of the truly atrocious state of the roads it took us 21 hours to go and 38 hours to return. "It is easy to tell someone to come to Nyankunde for an operation, but you need to understand the journey you are asking them to undertake," Helen explained.

The tropical rain forest is beautiful, and the rivers spectacular and frequent. At the same time, one has to see the mud holes with one's own eyes to believe them: there is no bottom to the mud! Although the road was built using hard core, wherever that hard core is breached you drive into a sea of mud, large marshy areas, knowing that there is no way you will reach the other side. Once well and truly stuck you block the road so the next person can't drive into the gumbo. They will then pull you out with winches and a cable before the next truck drives in. Every now and then the chauffeur with the best ropes or cables gets through and simply takes off, leaving those left behind to negotiate franticly about the subject of replacement hawsers.

The first leg of the journey took us to Lolwa, a mere 120 km away. We radioed the missionaries there to expect us, and when we didn't arrive Lester Green realized there must be a problem at the mud hole he knew existed a few kilometers from town. He showed up with a team of Pygmies who pushed us through.

There were no road signs or village names, but by dead reckoning and the help of that indispensible aid to African travel, the Michelin map, we had some idea where we were. On the map the road was marked with a deep red line, and looked wide and straight—a veritable boulevard! The reality on the ground was altogether different. Our chauffer, a Mr. Basuana, hadn't a clue about maps. He had been this way before and remembered the road; a line on a piece of paper held no meaning for him.

Other than the odd disabled truck with people camping beside it and, of course, at mud holes, other vehicles were a rare sight. Whenever we met a vehicle coming from the opposite direction we would stop and ask "Habari ya njia?" How is the road? Responses varied, but the most important one pertained to bridges, as in: "There is a bad bridge 19 kilometers away but you will get through fine in your small Toyota."

One treats bridges in Congo with respect. Before crossing, one stops and inspects the bridge's state. You will have to decide where best to place your tires, and rearrange some planks accordingly. Many of the bridges are old "bailey" bridges that were given to the Congo by the British government. The advantage of this type of bridge is that it easily spans rivers, without recourse to large winches and hoists, and can cover any particular span. Congolese bridges are not repaired until they break. The main bridge spanning the Ituri River on the main road across central Africa, the highway from Mombasa on the Indian Ocean to Lagos, Nigeria, once collapsed when a main support gave way, leaving half the bridge a twisted mass of metal. It took almost two years to repair it, during which time local people constructed barges that would take vehicles across for a price. Trucks or buses had to be completely unloaded or the barge would sink. Even so, some young fellows were kept busy bailing as the barge was pulled by ropes from one side to the other.

We had to take the ferry across the Napopo River. It was a well built, timber structure floating on empty oil drums. By orienting the ferry at just the right angle to the current, water power alone pushed it across in both directions. A cable strung across the river kept the contraption from drifting downstream.

We stopped at various churches on the way, all of which gave us a warm welcome and a meal. The biggest welcome was at Nebobongo hospital, where Helen had started her missionary career. The most important thing that Helen taught us was an attitude to the Africans that was very different from that of the former colonialists, the Belgians and, sadly, also different from that of many of the missionaries. Helen loved them and treated them as equals; it is amazing how much the attitudes of those around us affect us without our realizing it.

The Belgians had instituted a system that was like apartheid. In most big towns there were two hospitals, one for whites one for blacks. There were separate schools for whites and blacks. In Bunia the blacks lived on one side of a small river and whites on the other side. This may have subconsciously influenced many missionaries, who tend to hold their African brothers and sisters at arm's length. Helen, on the other hand, had learned the secret of being one in Christ during her 21 year missionary career. Through her contact with local pastors and people like John Mangadima she had developed a deep appreciation and love for the Africans, something she communicated to us during our time of orientation with her.

I was amazed—and frightened—by the wide range of surgical needs making their way to the hospital. I was pouring with sweat as I faced some extremely difficult surgical problems. Five years of training in general surgery cannot prepare you for the scope of surgery one faces in rural Africa. I felt particularly underprepared in the area of Gynecology; it was only later that Dr Ruth Dix, a gynecologist at Nyankunde, would give me some training in this area. I operated on a woman with huge fibroids after venereal disease—but the things were so stuck that I closed her back up without fully excising the problem. Another time I was left amazed at the apparent health of an older man from whom I removed a large length of gangrenous bowel. This was also the first time I met John Mangadima, the nurse surgeon at Nebobongo. He had trained as a nurse at Nebobongo, and then at Nyankunde, under Helen, and was doing a very good job with all the common forms of surgery that came to him.

After the original orientation trip with Helen, I was keen to see more of the rural hospitals and dispensaries in the area, and started dreaming about doing a motorbike trip through the area—I could excuse the adventure as being part of my orientation to the region! The trip was realized later that year when John Mangadima invited me along for a 1600 km. trip through the eastern Congo to visit a number of rural clinics and a small hospital. "We only have room for a small bag for your personal belongings," he warned me. "We need to carry all our own fuel as well as basic medical supplies." Soon we were off for our month-long journey with a couple of shirts, some socks and a spare pair of trousers in a satchel strapped to the back of the bike. What joy to be welcomed each evening by members of some church who were only too happy to supply whatever we needed, and do our laundry to boot! Without me having to say anything John ensured there was a bucket of water that had been heated over a wood fire in which I could wash up. Oh the sheer delight of a sponge bath after a long, dusty, sticky day on the road! Bathrooms ranged from an old missionary house now occupied by local pastors to a reed-walled enclosure outside. In only one place were there resident missionaries where I could sleep between sheets; elsewhere it was a blanket and a foam mattress.

Nor have I ever had a greater appetite! We'd arrive so hungry I enjoyed whatever was set before me. I gave up asking what it was, as the reply was either in a language I didn't know or I was told, "Eat up! We'll tell you afterwards." I believe I ate snake, monkey, insects and various grubs.

We met with the sick and helped or advised as best we could. Then, when there were no more patients to see or problems to try to understand, we'd move on to the next place. Even though our African hosts may have heard that we were coming, they were sensible enough not to make any preparation until they saw the whites of our eyes. We rarely needed to know the time—the only thing we needed to figure out was how much daylight was left, and my watch was of little use in this. I took it off on the second day. Based on the position of the sun we would decide if there was time to push on, or if we should head for the nearest church. The trip allowed me to pepper John with questions. "If my missionary life is like a motor car, what do you think is the axel that holds everything together?" I once asked him.

"Money," he replied. I was a bit disappointed with his answer, but it was borne out of contact with the many western missionaries who unwittingly absorbed the capitalistic mentality of their home countries.

The relationship I built with John during that carefree month was worth far more than the minor privations or sore backsides from long hours on an overloaded bike on unbelievably bad roads.

The various Africans who have stayed with us were another invaluable source of orientation. At various times we hosted Congolese nurses who were unable to find accommodation, as well as medical students and new graduates who came to gain practical experience. We inevitably gained more from this hospitality than we could give.

"We cannot understand why you have an African living with you," one of the Nyankunde church elders once commented. Kimp was unable to find a place to stay when he had to leave the dorm after graduation. He came from some distance away, and there was no one from his tribe in the area on whom he could lean. Our colleague, Dr John Harris, was willing to train and employ him in the leprosy service—if he could learn English. So we invited him to come and live with us, an arrangement which proved to be mutually advantageous: we learned more Swahili and French, and Kimp improved his English. He also gave us the inside story of the goings on in the school and hospital. He eventually joined the leprosy work, married, and the Leprosy Mission enabled them to buy a small cottage.

When Helen first arrived at Nyankunde she got Dr. Becker to agree that she could build a typical African mud hut for herself. That was the house we "inherited". It was not, in fact, a typical mud hut, though it looked like it from a distance. The basic frame of the hut consisted of wooden poles sunk two feet into the soil. It had a grass roof. Walls were made of poles bridged with thick stems of elephant grass plastered with mud. We were very pleased that from the outside the place looked very similar to scores of other mud huts; she and we tried very hard not to distance ourselves from the local population, and we also found that traditional building techniques had much to commend themselves. The fifteen inches of grass thatch made it a cooler house than many others, and the constant stream of Africans attested that they were not the least intimidated on coming into our dwelling. Admittedly, it was better finished and equipped on the inside. The windows had louvered glass and mosquito netting. It had a cement floor, running water, a cement bath and a flush toilet. The septic bed to the side of the house ensured that the pawpaw trees there grew well. There was only a single electrical outlet, but we managed quite comfortably, as the electric supply was spotty at best. There was a small vegetable patch and, in front, a small flower garden which boasted a beautiful Queen Elizabeth pink rose Helen had carried with her from the UK. It flowered all year long. The place wasn't Buckingham Palace, but a great place for a newly married couple to start life. In the course of time I took cuttings from that rose all over the place; there are now pink roses gracing many lawns across North-Eastern Congo.

Our days normally started at 6:30 A.M. with prayers in the hospital. That may sound early, but we lived just one degree north of the equator, meaning that every day of the year the sun always rises at 6 A.M. and sets at 6 P.M. (there was some slight variation from time to time; an eminent geographer once informed me that that was because the world "wobbles" a little). We made the most of daylight, and went to bed early. I have no idea how Dr. Becker persuaded the African staff to be on time, as punctuality is not a highly prized social value. Nevertheless he managed to get everyone together at the appointed hour for a short devotion and prayer. If we were ever late he would look pensively at his watch and ask, "Oh you were up late last night were you?" Mortified, you vowed never to be late again.

For some mysterious reason the devotional had to be given by a doctor—and we were all expatriates. I'm not sure how anyone profited from my bad Swahili back then. After prayers we did the ward rounds which, for me, meant visiting all the patients I had operated on. No one was in a hurry to leave the hospital. "Your hernia operation yesterday went very well, you can go home today."

"Oh no doctor, I want to stay until the stitches come out." For those who came from far away, which many did, this was a legitimate request. Those from local villages, however, enjoyed their stay in hospital, during which time their relatives had to feed them, and did not expect any work of them. It was one great holiday camp! Back then we only charged 10c a day for a bed, so people were in no hurry to leave. It is $2 a day today, but they are still not in a hurry.

After doing the rounds I'd head home for a quick breakfast of hot porridge made from local grains (corn, sorgum, soya or a mixture of different flours) and a mug of Robusta coffee. Then it was off to the operating room. There was always a long list of people who had arrived but had not yet had surgery. I might be doing a hernia, a lipoma, prostatectomy, hysterectomy, bone pinning or some form of bowel surgery. I tried to teach as much as possible to a Congolese colleague as I went about my business. Back then we did not have an anesthetist so we did as much as possible under local or regional anesthetic, and I would have to mentally monitor the patient as we went along. While I was operating away, Nancy was in the outpatient department dealing with those whom the nurse did not feel capable of treating.

Lunch was the main meal of the day. We had a full time cook, Benj, who also looked after the house while we were working. Initially he served western food—roast beef and potatoes kind of stuff—but in time we ate more and more of the local food.

Benj was kept very busy. Fruit and vegetables arrived at the door but had to be bartered for. Fresh milk came from a local herdsman, but needed to be sieved to remove the straw and then boiled to kill the TB bacteria. He'd let milk stand overnight, and then skim off the cream, which he would churn into butter. Meat came from the local open air market, but was minced at home. The laundry also needed to be done, and the garden tended. Beside Benj we usually employed a second fellow as well. Nancy once calculated that the bananas we harvested from our garden was sufficient to cover one of their salaries.

Afternoons were spent teaching in the nurses training college. The educational system in Congo leaned heavily on the memorization of class notes and their regurgitation during examinations. Our challenge was to make the teaching as practical as possible. We might spend our evenings preparing for teaching the next day or listening to a sermon on cassette tape. Occasionally we hosted another missionary family, or were invited out. Back then I enjoyed listening to the BBC World Service, in spite of spotty short-wave reception. Later we had a satellite radio with excellent reception. However, the internet soon made the satellite radios obsolete, even though internet service is still very difficult to find in many parts of Africa. Before tumbling exhausted into bed we'd take a bath or, later, a shower using the solar heater I hauled across the Sahara during my first overland crossing. Taking a shower is much more enjoyable when the hot water is free; I must have some Scot's blood coursing through my veins.

Excursion 4: "Blessed are the poor for theirs is the kingdom of God."

I need to come to terms with Jesus' statement to his recently appointed disciples, "Blessed are the poor for theirs is the kingdom of God" (Luke 6:20). It is difficult to imagine a more startling beginning to Christ's teachings on money than these words. "You will be happy if you are poor," he says.

Biblical Greek has two words for poor. First of all is "penes", which refers to people who have nothing superfluous to their basic needs, and have to work for a living. From this word we get the English word 'penury'. However, Luke uses "ptochos", which describes someone who is absolutely destitute. In other words, Jesus said "Blessed are the destitute", or "Happy are those who have to beg for a living."

The great philosopher Socrates was proud to be penes. He was proud of the fact that he earned his own living, that he did not require the largess of any relative or friend. On the other hand he describes ptochos, begging for a living, as shameful. In Greek literature the word ptochos was invariably used in a derogatory sense—until Luke tells us that Jesus used it to describe a state of blessing. The frantic pursuit of wealth in today's society indicates that few people believe this prescription for happiness. Their skepticism forces us to ask what Jesus was really getting at.

I believe that Jesus had a bias towards the poor. After stating in Luke 6:20 that the poor are blessed, he goes on to describe the woes the rich will inherit. Several times Luke records Jesus telling stories which begin with "There was a rich man", and every time the individual in question comes off badly, is criticised for his actions, and offered a bleak future. He also records Mary singing about the fact that God satisfies the poor with good things but sends the rich empty away (Luke 1:53).

The World Bank now fixes poverty at $1.90 a day, and finds that worldwide 12.7% of the population falls below this level, or 42.7% of the population of sub-Saharan Africa. Furthermore, poverty is growing. Back in 2004 the estimate was of 984 million people at or below the poverty line which, back then, was set at $1.-.[4] Not until I arrived in the Congo did I first meet really, really poor people. According to many estimates the

---

[4] World Bank Development Indicators: Poverty headcount ration. 2011.

Congolese are among the poorest in the world—although they live in a country that ought to be the richest in the world! Congo has remarkable natural resources: gold, diamonds, oil, cobalt, coal, rain, water, potential hydroelectric power, hard woods and immense agricultural potential. The Gross National Product of Congo is expected to rise by 9.3% a year. However, all of this wealth is controlled by a very small proportion of the population. And unlike many countries, where the government has established some kind of social security network, the wealth of Congo does not filter down to the man on the street, or the man in his small grass hut.

For instance, soldiers tell us that although their salaries may be sent out from Kinshasa, they are creamed off by the upper echelons in the army and do not arrive to those in the bush. Even though the Prime Minister is trying to correct this problem by having salaries paid directly into soldiers' accounts, with so few functioning banks around a soldier's salary can sit in an account more than 250 km away, over almost impassable roads from where he is stationed. Little wonder many groups of soldiers have deserted to form one of the many rebel groups who live by their guns in the north-east of the country. But... how poor is the population of the Congo really?

Few rural Congolese will handle as much as $100.- cash per year. They survive by bartering. Everyone can have a garden; you simply apply to the local chief to be given a piece of land. It may be some distance from your house, but can be quite large. You will need to clear and till it by hand. This is hard work. In the lush jungle the weeds grow as fast as the crops, so even if you can grow three crops of corn a year, you will have to do a lot of weeding. Soap is made from palm oil and ashes. The sap of some trees is combustible, and used as a source of light at night. Cooking is done over three stones using wood from the forest: mahogany, and African teak!

The growing season is year-round, so you do not need to store food, as there is always something growing in your garden. You don't need to plan for winter as there is no such thing. Of course your house does not need to be insulated. In rural areas, where everyone knows everyone else, there is no need to lock your door. In urban areas, however, theft is common. Your house has to have windows with shutters that are too tight for thieves to squeeze through.

This takes us to a secret of happiness: in a rural village everyone knows everyone else, and many people are related to each other. All the members of these extended families stay in touch, and share what they have. In fact, every normal, healthy human being finds greater pleasure in good relationships with one's spouse, children, grandchildren and fellow church members, than in money. Divorce invariably brings huge amounts of stress and unhappiness to both partners and their children. In a Congolese village everyone not only knows everyone else, they care for each other as well. Of course there are dysfunctional relationships, and conflict between clans or tribes can spill over into physical confrontation. On the whole, however, the Congolese are a very friendly and peaceable people. Furthermore, they are surrounded by natural beauty, the sun, the rain, lush gardens, and wild life. They can appreciate the simple things in life and rejoice over what they have. So... are they really impoverished?

One of the saddest things I have seen is a home for 350 homeless men in Toronto, Canada. These men cannot really be considered poor in financial terms: they have a room, bathroom, three meals a day and social security payments. They are there because of drug, alcohol or psychiatric problems. Life for many is spent on a balcony smoking. Conversation is sparse and laced with sexual and religious epithets – the "F" and "J" words. I was assisting in a research project to help the men write a "living will": in the event that they were incapacitated and could no longer make decisions about their medical care, who did they want to make decisions for them? Almost all of them were divorced, so a typical answer might be: "I want my girlfriend Darlene to decide for me."

"OK. What is Darlene's last name?" I'd ask.

"I'm not sure... I think I have her telephone number somewhere..."

Here was a "community" of people whose closest acquaintances were casual contacts they knew virtually nothing about—yet willing to put their lives in their hands!

Another fact that saddened me was learning that about a third of these homeless men had been to university. The root of their poverty was not financial, it was the fact that they had, somehow, become excluded from society, shunted off to the edge, even though they had received housing and social security benefits. Sadly, even in mainstream North American society, people are increasingly isolated from each other. They go to the library and check out books without saying a word to anyone. They draw money from an ATM without having to greet a bank teller. They sit at a computer or in front of a TV in the isolation of a multi-storey apartment block...

My point is that real poverty and real wealth can best be measured in terms of a sense of belonging, of happy relationships, and not in terms of dollars and cents. How delightful when my son wants to take me out for a father's day meal, or when I can have a few days with my grandkids, or take a holiday with my wife. I greatly value my relationship with fellow church members, I have friends on various committees I am a part of, and I enjoy classes at the 50+ lectures in the local university. Happiness comes from relationships not money; many Africans were happy and content until we provoked them to jealousy with overblown descriptions of the technology and the labour saving devices we enjoy over here.

Of course it is impossible to live in most parts of the world without money. Churches and mission agencies need money to function. However, we westerners seem to need material things for their own sake. We must not expect that money can buy happiness except in the very short term.

Happiness comes from being in right relationships with others, from being part of a larger group, family or "kingdom". It comes not from living in the "splendid isolation" only wealth can buy, but in being part of a living, sharing, loving community. In fact, the depth of our relationships are revealed when there is separation or death. "He who eats alone dies alone" is a Jewish proverb. God said, "It is not good that man should be alone" (Genesis 2:18).

Blessed are the poor for theirs is the kingdom of God. Jesus emphatically asserts that the "poor" can manifest that deep hope and trust in God which leads to eternal joy. The rest of the "Sermon on the Mount" is all about our relationships with each other and with God.

5

Travels in the Garden of Eden

THE GRASSLANDS of eastern Congo stretch far to the hills on the horizon. The tall elephant grass is burnt off in the dry season to allow young succulent shoots to grow as fodder for the nomadic peoples' cow herds. The nomads live in grass huts, the inner framework of which is made of the longest and stoutest grass stems and then thatch is added down to ground level. There is one hut for every adult in the family: one for the man and one for each of his wives and their children. The Belgians tried to outlaw this type of house because rats build their nests in the thatch, and rats are carriers of the bubonic plague. Every so often the "black death" still breaks out in this corner of Congo.

At the age of 11 a boy will start guarding his father's herd. He will earn a cow a year, so by the age of 21 he should have 10 cows. This will enable him to marry, as that is the usual bride price. Then, of course, he will be broke and will need to continue working for his father until he has built up his own herd again.

A few miles further takes us to the lip of a long hill. The scenery changes radically. The grass is gone and all you can see is what looks like broccoli tops: the tropical rain forest. There is no evidence of roads or houses below the canopy, no sign of life at all. And yet there is more life in the many layers of the jungle than anywhere else on earth.

The first time I drove through the forest I took a corner and splashed into a rocky stream. I wondered if I had missed a turn but, no, this was the road, the wide red line marked on the map. I followed the stream down a long incline to the bridge across the Ituri River. The bridge is just a single truck-width, and although the river can swell to 100 meters wide, it has just one support in the middle of the river. One of the most important of the many rules to bear in mind when driving in Congo is to treat every bridge with the utmost of respect. Because it is a mere truck-width we will not meet anyone halfway, so it will not have to carry the weight of more than a single vehicle at a time. A large sign states 'Maximum 25 tons'—but having traveled several hundred kilometers to get this far are you going to turn back if you weigh more?

The bridge will not receive any maintenance until one or another end drops into the water, so we proceed gently. We are on the lookout for crocodiles; there are probably hippos around as well. Disappointingly, thus far we have not seen any wild-animals. You could be 10 meters from a forest elephant and not see him for all the lush vegetation.

On the far side of the bridge, a ridge of grass runs down the middle of the road. Passing trucks have shaved it down so that it resembles a long crew-cut. This is very good! It means previous travelers did not have to leave the twin gullies created by many tires to avoid some mud hole. Unfortunately, other parts of the road look like a ploughed field leaving you slipping this way and that until you grind to a halt, axles buried in the mud. When you get stuck someone will eventually help out. Since people cannot pass you on the one lane 'highway', everyone lends a hand to everyone else so that they can move on as soon as you are out of the mud hole. It is difficult to describe mud holes. They seem to have no solid bottom; there is nothing firm below your feet as you venture to walk across.

Another danger are shifts in one's load. A cattle clunker filled with pigs pulls up and starts listing dangerously as all the animals are thrown to one side. There is only one thing to do: unload the truck, tying the pigs together by their tails so they don't run away, get the truck onto firm ground, then try and catch the beasts and reload.

One thing you learn through bitter experience is to be aware of huge bamboo stems alongside the road. Often 15 cm in diameter, the fast growing plant loves marshy areas. However, its thick foliage close to the ground keeps the mud from drying in spite of the intense equatorial sun.

The one advantage of the mud and pools of water is the abundance of butterflies they attract. Turquoise-spotted Swordtails are abundant, and often the size of your hand. No pesticides here! For that same reason be sure you don't get caught outside in the evenings, when the myriads of mosquitoes launch their nocturnal attacks.

Sometimes a group of nomadic pygmies will show up. They can build their simple green leaf shelters in minutes, and just as easily abandon it as they follow game. One member of the group is charged with carrying fire in a smoldering log. Although we may teach these short people to aspire another way of life, they must just as often consider us stupid for spending vast amounts of energy dragging our machines (trucks) through their territory. When they run into a "party" wrestling to get their truck out of the mud they will most likely stand to one side to observe and giggle. They would see no point in lending a hand.

These "Little People", or "premiers citoyens", are Africa's original inhabitants, the autochthones who, just like the "First Nations" of North America, have been treated badly in the past. Never taller than four foot six inches, these graceful, fun loving people are a joy to meet. With their fine features, few skin blemishes, and wearing just a bark skin loin cloth, most look healthy and sturdy. Even if they have few facilities to practice Western style hygiene, they remain free from most illnesses because they are mobile; they never stay in one place long enough for a significant number of pathogens to build up in the soil. Attempts have been made to get them to settle down along the roads so they can be counted (and taxed), but such experiments result in tuberculosis or worse. If a pygmy is ever hospitalized we doctors have a challenge on our hands. Because they are not used to being confined by four walls they will immediately discharge themselves from hospital.

We are in a small plane above the clouds, at least a 100 miles from the nearest road. The pilot spots a hole in the cloud cover, descends through it and we fly just over the canopy of trees. We pass over a small clearing and see pygmy huts invisible at normal cruising altitudes.

Although the forest is alive with wild things, one has to look carefully to see it, even at ground level. You may, for instance, notice a 4 centimeter brown line crossing the path. The outside of this line does not move; it consists of large army ants facing outwards. In between them is a mass of smaller ants all traversing the track in the same direction. If you step on the line of ants they will sink their jaws into your skin. You will have to pick every single ant out of your flesh. If you drive over the line hundreds of ants will die, but the line will quickly reform.

Movement in the top of the 100 meter trees may signal the presence of a troop of Macao monkeys. The only evidence of larger animals, like elephants, are the large turds, left maybe just minutes earlier as they quickly blended into the dense forest when they heard the vehicle approach. Once when we rounded a sharp bend we came across a giant, bright blue bird, the rare and beautiful Blue Coraco found almost exclusively in Congo. According to the students accompanying me they are very tasty!

Another animal unique to Congo is the shy Okapi. It has the backside of a zebra, the body of a horse, the neck of a giraffe, the head and ears of an antelope, and is the size of a large donkey. I have never heard of anyone running into a wild Okapi.

The Congo is rich in minerals. I once visited a gold mine with some students. Ore from deep below the ground was crushed, and then washed over a shaking table over troughs lined with coconut matting. The washings of gold were amalgamated with mercury to make nuggets, to be sent away for further purification. There were no end of rumors about this gold. One story suggested that Switzerland refused to accept any more gold in Mobutu's personal name in case he removed it all at once, and so embarrassed the Swiss financiers.

Once we visited the Virunga national park, an amazing reserve in the central African rift valley stretching from the tropical rain forest to the eternal snows on Mount Rwenzori. Established in 1925, it is Africa's first national park. It became a UNESCO-designated World Heritage Site in 1979. We saw numerous animals: herds of buffalo, elephants and no end of hippos. Since the wars that started in 1994, however, the number of animals has reduced significantly.

Another time we visited Ishangu, a small village on the northern edge of Lake Edward. The lake abounds with fish. The fishing boats were surrounded with greedy pelicans, and the villagers had no end of delicious barbequed fish available to sell to us.

The "Blue Mountains" to the west of Lake Albert run roughly from the north to the south. Although not very high, they marked the start of the Congo for East Africa's early explorers. Few ventured in, partly because travel became very difficult on the far side of the mountains due to vegetation, rivers and marshes, and because navigating is very difficult when you can only see a few feet in front of you. Many maps made at the end of the eighteenth century simply labeled the west side of the mountains as "unknown territory". Henry Morton Stanley was the first to bring the Congo to the attention of Europe. Because of the backing he received from King Leopold of Belgium, the Congo became the Belgian Congo.

Towards the end of the 19th century Stanley crossed west to east through the Congo. It was a grueling journey which took the lives of more than half his party. Eventually he climbed a hill not far from Nyankunde and caught a glimpse of the grass lands of East Africa, with which he was familiar. It is easy to sense the relief he must have felt to step out of the hot, dense jungle through which he had to slash a path, and into open territory. He camped below the Blue Mountains for six months to recuperate from his trek through the jungle. We once took our students into these mountains, passing the cement memorial indicating the site where Stanley recovered. At the top of the escarpment is another memorial stone. This one indicates the watershed in the middle of Africa. Rain water to the west drains down into the Congo River and to the Atlantic, while the other side drains into Lake Albert, which is part of the headwaters of the Nile that drain out into the Mediterranean.

The sight of Lake Albert, a huge body of water, always surprised the students. Most had never seen so much water, even though many of them lived fairly close by.

Traveling overland in the Congo is an act of faith as there are neither fuel stations nor repair shops in the jungle. We have developed the habit of praying before we set out for good reason, as there is much that can go wrong. It is amazing how often these prayers for a safe trip have been answered.

Once a brake seized up in the middle of the jungle, but we continued driving with abandon until a passenger noticed black smoke wafting from one of the front wheels. We ground to a halt as flames starting licking round the tire. While we doused the flame a crowd began to gather. Amazingly, an African nurse with us spotted a casual acquaintance in the crowd whom he knew to be a chauffeur. The man disconnected the hydraulic line and sealed it with a nail. In no time we were on our way, though with braking power to only 3 of the 4 wheels.

Land Rovers are amazing vehicles. Because they are bolted together it is relatively easy to approach any part of the power train. One disadvantage of this accessibility, however, is that all those bolts work loose on rough terrain. Old Land Rovers in Africa create an awful rattle. If you provide your passengers with a screwdriver they are kept occupied for the duration of the trip.

Once we experienced a complete loss of power. We soon learned that the flywheel had separated from the clutch plate. Six bolts, now mangled, had worked loose. What was the chance of finding replacements when one is 2,000 km from the nearest dealer? However, in the workshop of the Roman Catholic Mission up the road we found a Land Rover engine that was being cannibalized for spare parts, found the requisite six bolts, reconnected the flywheel, and kept travelling.

A barrel of fuel gets you some ways away from home, but not necessarily back again. Such fuel as arrives in central Africa is generally sold to the highest bidder and is rarely, if ever, obtainable at a gas pump. Having local friends whom you know to visit when you need fuel helps a lot. Missionaries depend on God and others to provide everyday supplies in a way that most middle-class westerners take for granted.

Sometimes we would take trips to isolated areas, places where there were no medical facilities at all. We would have to take everything we would need with us: sterilizer, drapes, surgical instruments, medicines, as well as everything we needed to keep the vehicle going. Once a student with a basic knowledge of English asked if the "Stop Leak" fluid you could add to the radiator in case it sprung a leak was medicine for diarrhea!

Upon arrival we would look for a room we could turn into an operating theatre. It might be the primary school or maybe just a mud hut with a cement floor. We'd find a school teacher with a watch, and teach him or her how to use the sterilizer (autoclave). After that we'd recruit some women to wash and dry the operating room linens. One of our students would show someone else how to fold the materials to put in the autoclave. Then, after consulting everyone who thought they needed an operation, we would be ready to start.

The operating table consisted of any convenient table, and anesthesia was local whenever possible and, if not, regional (spinal). One student would be monitoring vital signs during anesthesia. There was usually a minor panic soon after we'd started when we discovered we'd forgotten something important, but in general it is amazing what you can do with the minimum of equipment in simple surroundings.

When the Leprosy Mission gave Nebobongo hospital a brand new Land Rover, I volunteered to drive it overland from London to Congo across the Sahara desert. Dr. Dave Burnett, who was just starting a career at All Nations College, was eager to go with me.

We packed the vehicle with medical supplies that were difficult to obtain in Congo, including an operating room light in a big, black crate which looked just like a coffin. We strapped it onto the roof rack; it really facilitated several border crossings. Just before our send-off from Guildford Baptist Church the insurance company informed us that they had made a mistake, and that we needed to pay an extra 256 pounds. We had emptied our bank account, and simply didn't have the extra money. The pastor, David Pawson, mentioned our need to the people that had met to see us off, and the money collected came to exactly 256 pounds! This would prove to be the first of many blessings.

Someone else strolled up to us. "It looks to me as though your vehicle is listing badly to the right," he said in a west-country accent. What with all our goods on board we had broken a spring before we'd even got going! "I'll fix you up with my Land Rover specialist in Alton," Harold Wakeford promised. We postponed our departure by 24 hours, during which the garage installed appropriate heavy duty springs—no doubt the reason why the Rover held up to those awful Congolese roads for more than ten years.

We managed to cross the Sahara in a little over three weeks. The road had a tar macadam finish right up to Tamanrasset, in southern Algeria, although in places there were many potholes. To our amazement, the road had been washed away in one place in the middle of the desert by a flash flood. After Tamanrasset we were supposed to join a convoy and register our departure with the police. We linked up with a young couple in a similar, though older, Land Rover. In the low hills just outside of town the track was cursed with unending "corrugations", or regular transverse bumps built up by the shifting of loose gravel and sand by rebounding vehicles with bad shock absorbers. You either go slow to preserve your vehicle or you take them fast to minimize the discomfort but at the risk of breaking a spring. Our companions took them fast, and we took them slowly. That was the end of our "convoy".

The road here is marked by an oil barrel every half kilometer, and you don't leave one barrel until you can see the next for fear of getting lost. An ever present danger is to get caught in a depression filled with fine drifting sand, danger points often marked by half submerged abandoned cars which, because there is little or no rain, still have immaculate paint work. "Capetown or bust": they busted...

The border crossing into Niger at Assamaka is both unusual and spectacular. There is a large, old stone fort on a high hill, from the side of which flows an artesian well. Warm gaseous water with a distinct sulfurous flavor coming from very deep down constantly bubbles out of a rusty old pipe protruding from the fort.

Every desert well is marked on the Michelin map along with a number stating the depth at which you can expect to find water. This can be important information, as you need to provide your own rope and pail. However, we had enough water with us that we didn't need to use any wells.

It was at the Niger border that a customs officer asked us to unpack the Rover completely: "Lay everything out on the sand." This would have been a huge job, but we obliged by unpacking a few things, including several pairs of second hand glasses. The custom officer tried on a pair. "Oh these fit fine. You can go now!"

We got stuck in a sand dune at midday that same day. Sand had blown across the track to make a dune about 20 meters high. We tried to drive up it quickly, but were soon stuck. We had to dig out the sand blocking the wheels, put in sand ladders, advance some 3 meters, and then start digging again. We had not dug for more than 10 minutes before we collapsed exhausted beside the vehicle. It was only then that, to our shame, we thought of praying about the situation. Less than 5 minutes later a small unladen Toyota Land Cruiser pulled up. Because it was empty it easily drove over the dune. Once on the other side the couple attached us to their winch and hauled us over. I am convinced they were angels God sent to help us.

Desert sand is more slippery in the heat of midday than at other times. We would have had much less trouble if we had not driven through the middle of the day, which is why the Algerian army only travels at night. To do that, however, you need to know the road well: if you wander off the track at night you are lost in no time. One sand dune looks just like another.

Some 600km after Tamanrasset we were back on a well finished road at Arlit, in northern Niger. Huge mounds of sand on the horizon marked the large uranium mines in the area. The road would remain quite good until we crossed over into the Congo.

As mentioned, the big wooden box on the roof was a great asset at another border crossing because it looked just like a coffin."What have you got up there?"

"Come and look." I would guide the customs officer up the short ladder at the back of the vehicle and prize open the lid.

"Oh it's just a lamp! Off you go."

We had really looked forward to a shower at a missionary guest house in Northern Nigeria, but they turned us away; maybe we looked too much like desert rats. We were nearly turned away from the missionary guest house in Bangui, Central African Republic, as well: "We are full with a special guest – Dr Stanley Browne, who is here giving a seminar".

"Oh could I please greet him? He is a long lost friend who visited us in Congo". They soon found a room and shower for us!

A ferry across the river at Bangasou was quite an experience. One imagines that people cross it all the time, but that is not the case. I had to negotiate for some time with the ferry captain, stationed on the Congolese side, traveling across the river in a dugout canoe paddled by a young boy. "Have you been to school?"

"Yes, I'm in third year primary."

"Your French is very good."

"I come from Central African Republic NOT Congo!"

After giving the ferry operator some of our precious diesel and the loan of our battery he eventually took us across. The roads in the Congo were worse than those in the desert, but we made it to Nebobongo from London in three weeks.

I would do the same trip again three years later in a larger truck. That time the journey proved to be considerably more difficult. Not only was the truck a bad choice for the terrain, its contents were a bigger problem. We carried a small container of equipment which had been sealed by British customs officers in Dover, but in Algeria the customs insisted they seal it a second time. However they also wanted us to post a bond in the UK, meaning we were stuck in Algiers for two weeks to deal with all the bureaucracy. Fortunately, some friends in the Algiers Anglican Church kindly put us up. At the Assamaka fort on the Niger border we received the same instruction as the previous visit. "Take everything out and lay it on the sand". We refused to do so.

"Fine, but then you will need to take a soldier with you all the way to the Nigerian border to make sure you don't unload any arms here in Niger, and then you will need to pay his return trip". Having a soldier on board proved to be a great blessing, for he knew the road well and directed us along the firmest track. This time we did not get stuck.

At the Nigerian border they insisted on breaking the seals and inspecting our cargo. The customs officer spotted a new pair of black shoes, which he confiscated, and then we were free to go. Once again the worst roads were in Congo. We had to leave the truck in north-west Congo until the dry season before we could drive it through to Nyankunde. Among the most important items in the container were commercial, stainless steel cooking stoves for the nursing school kitchen, which had used firewood between three stones to prepare food up to that point.

In the 1970's and 80's we went on a number of medical safaris in Mission Aviation Fellowship's small planes; an American foundation paid for these flights for a number of years. I liked to take my wife Nancy with me on these trips, as this enabled me to concentrate on the surgery. I would commonly do some 10 major surgeries a day, usually with two separate operating tables on the go. One team could finish up one case while we started on someone else. Later we took our children along on these trips. (Our son Jeremie was on 110 such flights before he stopped counting). Even though most were single-engine planes, and an emergency landing in the dense forest would be impossible, we never had any problems. The pilots were all trained mechanics who kept their machines in tip top condition, knowing that their own lives depended on their expertise.

Flying with a commercial airline was much less safe. I once needed to go to Kinshasa for business, and then on to a medical refresher course in Nairobi, Kenya. Nancy and the boys flew straight to Nairobi with MAF, while I bought a ticket with Ethiopian Airways from Kinshasa to Nairobi. When I showed up with my ticket they informed me they couldn't take me as the flight was full; a Chinese delegation had taken over the entire plane. "You can change your ticket at Air Zaire to fly with them."

Air Zaire had been described as a series of airplane parts flying in formation, but I had no choice. We landed at Mbuji Mayi, where some passengers got off, and others joined. Then we took off for Bujumbura. However, the pilot informed us that we had broken a shock absorber when landing in Muji Mayi, and that we would go to Goma instead, where they had the necessary parts. In Goma they had the necessary part but not the requisite tools. "We will go to Bujumbura where our friends at KLM will help us," the pilot announced. In Bujumbura they had tools but no parts. "We will ask a small plane to fly the parts from Goma. We will spend the night here, and leave for Nairobi in the morning." I arrived in Nairobi 24 hours late.

In the meantime, Nancy, Jeremie (5 ½ years old) and Timothy (2 ½ years old) were increasingly distressed. Daddy was expected Friday afternoon but did not come. Suppertime, no Daddy. Bedtime, no Daddy. They prayed for a safe arrival in the morning. Morning came, no Daddy. After breakfast the boys played outside on the swings and slides for awhile. Nancy contacted MAF Nairobi who had high frequency radio contact with MAF Congo. There was no news of a plane crash and no news of my being in prison for not having a Zaire visa in my passport. Somehow Nancy had that passport with her. Nancy contacted Ethiopian Airlines for their passenger list the day before. My name was not on it. Why had it been removed? Was this evidence of prison? Lunchtime, no Daddy. After lunch they prayed earnestly together that Daddy would come while they were having their afternoon sleep. When they woke from their sleep, Daddy was there. Cheers. Relief.

If you can, avoid flying in and around Equatorial Guinea. First of all, there was the inevitable mad rush for seats, as they issue far too many boarding passes. A soldier passed through the cabin to remove extra people, i.e., wherever three people had squeezed into two seats, one had to go. Then it started to pour with rain. The dripping baggage train with everyone else's baggage (I only had a carry-on) sat forlornly on the tarmac; no one tried to load the plane, so we left without any check-in luggage. There were still too many people on the flight, which would have been fine had it not stormed. To distract the passengers the pilot started playing some music over the intercom. As this was an old Russian Aeroflot plane, we were treated to a balalaika solo, which only seemed to increase the overall tension.

Once I was scheduled for the half hour flight from Bata to Douala, to catch a 3 PM flight to Nairobi. We left on time at 9 AM, but I still missed my connection! Instead of flying north, the plane turned south. "There is an important politician in Libreville we need to take to Douala." We landed in Libreville, picked up our man and taxied to the end of the runway, where the pilot revved the engines for 5 minutes. "There is a problem with this plane. You must all get off and wait in the transit lounge while we repair it." We were allowed to re-board two hours later, and we took off. "The plane still has a major problem. We need to go to Malabo to change planes." I arrived in Douala at 4 PM, an hour after my connecting flight had left. I had to wait for two days before I could travel on to Nairobi.

Our longest trip was in 1984, when we traveled around the globe. My sister, living near Los Angeles, had invited us over. It was cheaper to go round the world rather than to fly directly from Nairobi to Los Angeles and return. Together with our two boys, then aged eight and five, we flew from Nairobi to Bombay, then on to Delhi. From there we flew to Hong Kong, where we stayed the weekend with some old Cambridge friends. From Hong Kong we traveled to Hawaii, where we enjoyed two days on the beach. When we finally arrived in Los Angeles my sister took us to Disneyland. "You would never forgive yourselves if you knew how close you had been and had not visited the place," she explained.

After that we travelled up to San Francisco, and from there to Vancouver, Canada, where Nancy's parents met us. While the grandparents looked after the kids we took some church meetings, and then we traveled on to Calgary and Toronto, where we spent 4 weeks with our Canadian home church. On to Montreal, and from there to London, England, and our church in Guildford for another 4 weeks. Then it was on to Switzerland, to visit a doctor interested in work at Nyankunde. From there we flew to Jerusalem, where we spent five days, and then back to Nairobi. We did not lose a single piece of luggage all that way.

Trekking and travelling around eastern Congo was always an adventure, and the police only made it more so. We would pull up to a check point, where a policeman would look into our overloaded Land Cruiser. They obviously recognized that we were not locals. It was the end of the month, when school fees were due.

"You are not allowed to carry cargo on the back seat. I need to fine you. Five dollars please."

"Yes, I know you like to fine expatriates on the spot because they carry money around."

"Well you have been here long enough to know our rules!"

"True, so I also know how locals deal with your demands," and I handed him a one hundred franc note, the equivalent of about ten cents.

When they asked for my documents another time I handed over a large envelope stuffed with blue, green and pink papers, all bearing impressive cachets. "This is our registration, here is the insurance, our road tax, last year's insurance, our mechanical inspection..."

"OK, you can go." I had forgotten my driving license but, fortunately, the man did not notice. An observant student told me later that I had showed him all those papers upside down.

It is hard to escape the impression in the Congo that the police are there to serve themselves, not the population. "There are 64 road blocks between Wamba and Butembo," my taxi driver complained one day. That is a distance of about 500km.

You have to show your papers at each of these road blocks and, yes, you guessed it, they will always find something wrong for which you must pay a fine on the spot. These fines can be significant for a taxi driver; six dollars is not unusual. For my part, I try and hide behind the smoked glass, because some official may think I represent a tidy sum of money. "You need to be registered." Someone who is barely literate, who finds his way through your passport with great difficulty, scribbles in a scruffy notebook. "That will be five dollars." No receipts.

Corruption is an enormous problem in Congo, a result of the country's endemically poor administration. Many policemen have told us that as they receive no salary they have to fine people for imaginary offenses. Policemen are now among the richest people in the Congo, with most owning their own vehicles. Sometimes we have felt like "sheep among wolves" (Luke 10:3). Matthew adds that we need to be "as harmless as doves and as wise as serpents" (Mat. 10:16).

Once when I was on my way to a wedding we were stopped at a roadblock. Everything was in order—registration, insurance, technical inspection—except that my driver's license, which had no expiry date, still had "Zaire", printed on it. The country had had a name change. I began arguing with the policemen, determined not to pay him the fine because it would just disappear into his own pocket. I was sure we'd be late for the wedding, when he suddenly relented and let us go. I learned later that one of my Congolese passengers had slipped him $10 when I was not looking.

Before 1994 there had been a church movement called the "Chain of Honesty", which involved Christians choosing to wear a symbolic small gold chain in their lapel to indicate that they would not ask for or pay bribes. However, a Christian Congolese doctor whom I greatly respect told me at that time that he could not live in Congo without paying bribes. It was expected that he, as a Congolese, would fall in with the "system". We missionaries, as visitors in their land, might be treated slightly better, but he had to go along with the prevailing climate.

Everybody gets asked for bribes. An inspector of education from Kisangani once was honest enough to tell us how he had been caught. His salary had not been coming through from Kinshasa, so he was advised to go to the capital to sort out the problem. He managed to get as far as the computer room where the pay slips were printed. There the computer manager told him that they had run out of printer paper—a round-about way of asking for a bribe. The paper would have appeared by magic for the right bribe.

Things took a serious turn for the worse in 1994, when President Mobutu ran out of money to pay the army. He instructed his army to "Debrouillez-vous", meaning "help yourselves". The army looted Kinshasa, breaking into shops and walking off with televisions and stereos. Ever since then the country's underlying philosophy is that you are stupid if you don't use your position to enrich yourself. Look after yourself, for no one else will. It is particularly sad that a country which claims to be 90% Christian should be run this way. How different all this is from the teaching of Jesus, who taught us to have confidence that He would provide his children with the necessities of life, and who went so far as to give his own life on behalf of others.

Sadly, this mindset of (necessary) selfishness also spills over into the church. Once, during a seminar our hospital chaplain was giving to other chaplains, he presented them with a hypothetical scenario. "Suppose," he said, "that you were given $18 to buy a sheet of roofing material, and suppose that you could bargain it down to $15. What would you do with the remaining $3?"Almost unanimously they stated that this would be a blessing from the Lord. Each of them would have pocketed the 3 dollars. Fortunately, not everyone behaves like this. The Administrator of the Bunia nursing school had to buy 100 roofing sheets, for which he had budgeted $1800. He was able to get the sheets for $1500, and returned the extra $300 to the school.

If you insist on a receipt the vendor will assume that you want to reclaim this sum from your employer, so he will ask whose name you want on the receipt, and for how much he should make it out. Of course he knows how much you paid, but he wants to know what you think your boss would consider acceptable, and then you can keep the difference.

Every place I have ever been in Africa there are problems with land ownership. A mission agency once bought a house in Bunia, but after a year a family came from Kinshasa with papers that "proved" the house was theirs. According to them, the mission had paid the money to someone who was not the real owner of the property, and that the ownership papers he had given were forgeries. Now you can challenge this sort of thing in court, but there the result generally goes in favor of the one who paid the most money to the judge. Another property was lost when a builder claimed that the mission had never paid his now deceased father for a development project. The Mission agreed they had not paid, but stated that the project had never been undertaken. A local tribunal simply confiscated the property in exchange for what they said were the unpaid fees—even though a superior court had transferred the case to the regional capital, Kisangani.

When I was last in Kisangani I was impressed with all the new buildings going up there, only to discover that it was "the honorable so-and-so" investing money originally earmarked for road repairs. Corruption is so endemic that no one holds anyone accountable, because then they might themselves be held accountable. Despite the huge size of the Congolese church, few Congolese Christians are seeking to redress the problem.

Excursion 5: "What shall we do then?"

"What shall we do then?" was the question many who came to John the Baptist to be baptised asked. His answer was straightforward: "He who has two coats, let him share with him who has none; and he who has food, let him do likewise" (Luke 3:11). Practical advice, but not easy for most of us to follow, particularly for missionaries to one of the poorest nations on earth.

In Luke's version of the Sermon on the Mount, Jesus expands John's instructions: "From him who takes away your coat do not withhold even your shirt. Give to every one who begs from you; and of him who takes away your goods do not ask for them again. As you wish that men would do to you, do so to them" (Luke 6:28-31). These are challenging words! In practice this means we are to become extremely generous with our time, talents, money and possessions.

When tax collectors asked John what they should do he instructed them to collect no more than was appointed them (Luke 3:13). There are plenty of tax collectors in the Congo: road tax barriers on the roads, customs officers, and aviation authorities working at the airports, etc, etc., all telling you that "you need to pay!" And, of course, most of the money ends up in the pockets of the collectors; you do not receive any receipts, and if you do they do not add up to the sum paid, then the sum asked for varies from one day to the next. It is very difficult for outsiders to speak into the situation but, at the very least, the country needs to discipline both the giving and receipt of taxes. John said "Collect no more than is appointed you."

Soldiers also asked John what they should do, and he told them to "rob no one by violence or by false accusation, and be content with your wages" (Luke 3:14). Corruption includes the idea of misusing your position and authority to line your own pocket. Because the soldier's pay is not only low, but also it rarely filters through the system down to the ordinary soldier, soldiers are tempted to desert from the army and make a living by force of arms as small rebel groups. There are, we are told, now more than 40 such rebel groups in the north-east of Congo.

Even though we, personally, may not be acting in such destructive ways, John's answers are, nevertheless, instructive for us as well. Firstly, he asks us to be generous with what we have. Secondly, he urges us to be careful about what we accumulate. I know of missionaries who give away anything they have not used in the previous six months. I personally thank God for the very small apartment we have today, as it encourages us not to hoard. Thirdly, we are not to let our peers' bad materialistic life-styles influence us and, fourthly, we must learn to be content, even on low salaries.

Jesus constantly sought to encourage the poor on the one hand, and pointed out the pitfalls of being rich on the other. In today's society—and maybe throughout the ages—people have an inherent tendency to be drawn by the seductive lure of the power, pleasure, and security that are perceived as the by-products of wealth.

Jesus Christ, the co-creator and sustainer of all the earth's wealth, voluntarily left His Heavenly Father, to be born in a stable and fall under the tutelage of a simple carpenter. During his brief public ministry he quickly won the support of the commoners and the hostility of the rich and influential. His material needs during His itinerant ministry were met by the generosity of His followers: "Foxes have holes and birds of the air have nests, but the Son of Man has no place to lay his head," he testified (Luke 9:58). Centuries after His death, however, those who claimed to follow in his footsteps taxed the commoners to build great cathedrals in which to worship him. Something, somewhere, went terribly wrong...

The consequences of discipleship should be faith, hope and love, but these are contingent upon a renunciation of the subtle call of "things". In its most radical form this consists of a renunciation of finance altogether, so as to remove the possibility of conformity and absorption into a worldly view of money. However, we cannot live without an income in the modern world, so we must develop a right attitude to "things", to possessions.

In any discussion of poverty we must make a distinction between that which an individual needs to live and that which he merely desires to possess. We must differentiate between needs and wants. The United Nations defines poverty as "a denial of choices and opportunities"[5], meaning a lack of the basic capacity to participate effectively in society. Once again we find ourselves invoking the idea of relationships rather than the simple possession of money. Poverty means more than not

---

[5] UNDP Human Development Report 1997.

having enough to feed and clothe a family, or not having a school or clinic to go to, or not having the land on which to grow one's food, or a job to earn one's living, or not having access to credit, even though these are elements in the total equation.

The world's poor are very aware of the enormous choice of foods, clothing, entertainment, houses or cars that the wealthy enjoy. It makes them feel poor, even though they may still have access to the basics, as well as family structures that enable everyone in them to find their place and feel accepted. Basically, many of the world's poor are envious of "stuff" that they, and we, don't really need. In fact, the pursuit of the "stuff" often leads to the loss of close family structures—it may be that, in this sense, the poor are often richer than the wealthy.

Rich or poor, we all have to wrestle with two important, interrelated questions: to what extent is "my" money in reality something the donor, God, wants me to use on his behalf, as his steward? And if that is the case, what does he want me to invest in?

6

Snapshots

The Family Home

A CHURCH in the UK which prayed for us on a regular basis once informed us they felt led to pray specifically that Nancy get pregnant—not something we had ever mentioned in one of our letters. Well, within a month Nancy was expecting! She received excellent care from an American midwife serving at the clinic 100 yards from our African hut. She also attended the prenatal clinic at the hospital with all the other pregnant African mothers. Living right next door to us was our obstetrician, Dr. Ruth Dix, who helped Nancy through the delivery two weeks before the due date. I was not overly enthusiastic to be present at the birth—I know everything that can go wrong—but when the delivery was imminent I received a summons to appear. Jeremie was a placid addition to our family, a real gift from God.

We had had to wait for some time for Nancy to be pregnant with Jeremie, so were taken by surprise when she became pregnant again just 9 months later! This time, however, labor started 10 weeks before Nancy was due. Jonathan Peter was tiny when he was born. He had breathing problems from the start. We had no respirator or oxygen, and incubators existed only in an encyclopedia on the shelf. Jonathan died an hour after birth.

Many people supported us through that difficult time, and we were showered with love and sympathy from friends black and white. Although this was a traumatic experience, particularly for Nancy, it drew us closer to our African families. "Baba Butso", the senior elder in the church, remarked that he could not remember the last time a missionary family had lost a child, though this was all too common in African families. The event certainly cemented ties between us and those we had come to serve.

While in Toronto for a brief visit in 1980 to renew ties with family friends and supporting churches Nancy was pregnant again. We had planned to spend some time at Emmaus Bible Institute in Switzerland to improve our French and Biblical knowledge, as well as recuperate physically and mentally after seven years in the Congo, and saw no reason she could not have the baby there. Because of Nancy's obstetrical history, however, our doctor in Canada insisted we delay our departure for Switzerland until after the birth. We will always be grateful that he did so. Just days after making the decision to stay longer in Canada Tim wanted to come early, at 23 weeks, 17 weeks before he was supposed to. This would have been just days after we were supposed to be in Switzerland. We rushed to the hospital and by shouting, "my wife is having a baby" made it into a delivery floor in double-quick time. There I could explain that she was only 17 weeks along in her pregnancy, and that they had better start doing something to stop her contractions. Nancy was keen to breast feed, something that would be difficult to do if Tim was born before 36 weeks; she had to delay giving birth until 4 weeks before the due date. This involved two months of medications and laying in bed in obstetrical intensive care. At 36 weeks they stopped the medications and Nancy was allowed out of bed for the first time in several weeks in order to take a shower. We went to the hospital cafeteria for a meal together, and Tim was born 24 hours later.

Getting Nancy into the hospital had been no problem, getting her out again was a different story. She had spent a total of sixty-six days in the hospital, thirty-one of them in intensive care. The bill for medical care was well over $20,000.-. That was not the kind of money we had. When a very kind and well-off uncle heard that we had come from overseas and might not be covered by the government health insurance, he offered to pay the entire bill! Unknown to either him or us, however, we had already been approved for coverage following a previous medical consultation by a very astute specialist who had foreseen problems. Even our nonrefundable "bargain basement" tickets, which we thought we'd forfeited on Nancy's third day in hospital, were paid back because our travel agent refused to sell tickets that cheap and inflexible without insurance. Luck? Skillful planning on our part? Or divine provision? It was another instance of God's generosity: baby Tim traveled free, but was given a full baggage allowance.

Upon arrival back in the Congo in 1981, we needed a new house. The mud house we had inherited from Dr. Helen Roseveare was falling apart due to the loss of an inch of grass from the roof every year and the ravages of termites on the buried portions of the supporting poles. The new house would be much more permanent than our old one, and since most materials were available locally it need not be too expensive to build. In fact, a local builder assured us that he could build us a new "proper brick" house for $8,000. Clay would be pressed in a mould to make bricks which, once dry, would be baked in a kiln. Timber sawn in the forest a few miles away could be used for the roof, and the only really expensive items would be imported cement and iron roofing. We got on the man's waiting list, and remained on it for the next two years. When he was finally ready to start building he raised his estimate to $12,000, a daunting 50% increase. Then, when the bills started coming, it soon became obvious that even the second estimate was somewhat inadequate. This was when I started worrying about where the funds would come from: putting my no-worry theology into practice was not as easy as it sounds! When the final bills had been paid the project ended up costing $32,000! And yet, in spite of our fears and frustrations, the money came in through a variety of sources through whom, we are certain, God provided. One large gift came from a ranch in Alberta. We dashed off a thank you letter hoping there might be a follow-up donation, but our letter was returned "addressee unknown", so we never learned where that gift came from. We are sure, however, that it was prompted by the Lord, even as we remain extremely grateful to those who gave the donation yet did not receive any expression of gratitude.

Because the house was built on hospital land we knew that when we left it would be donated to the hospital. We enjoyed the place for six great years, and after us various and sundry people serving at the hospital have enjoyed living in it.

Most missionaries live on a limited budget. Our experience of God's provision does not mean going without so much as making the most of what you have. It will mean that all your needs are met but not necessarily all your wants. For instance, one's diet in the middle of Africa can get monotonous, and there are no restaurants offering anything interesting. As a result the *More with Less* cookbook became one of our prized possessions. It is amazing what a bit of this or that spice can do to a dish, and how stew can be turned into stroganoff, or fish into tandoori. I remember going to a missionary conference where we ate in groups. Although each cook was provided with the same basic ingredients for the evening meals, it was fascinating to see how each group managed to create different meals. One group might turn a can of sardines into a salad, another into fish pizza, and yet another into fish pie.

We once spent three days on a mission station doing some medical work with a couple of our nursing students. While they stayed with the senior pastor, we were billeted with the resident missionary couple. When we left we mentioned to the students that we would not miss the food we had been offered: corned beef salad one day, corned beef fritters the next day and, lastly, corned beef pie. "This is the best place we've been yet!" the students chimed. "Antelope one day, tortoise the next and then we had monkey meat!"

Congolese food tends to be very bland but, all the same, we have been glad for the services of a full time cook. After Nancy and I had been at work for most of the day we really did need someone to take care of kitchen and household tasks that do not need to be done in the West: milk needs to be boiled after straining to kill the tuberculosis bacilli, and then kept overnight to let the cream rise. It is churned into butter or ice cream. Our drinking water also needed to be boiled and filtered. Meat has to be minced and vegetables bought and washed carefully. Although African food is healthy in that there are no chemical additives or pesticides, infectious diseases are rife. One has to be very careful with anything that has not been boiled.

While the food may be simple, conversations around the table were generally stimulating. An African doctor we had staying with us insisted on bringing a small encyclopedia, the *Petite Larousse* and the Bible to the table so that we could explore any topics we broached in greater depth.

There were, of course, many aspects of western life that we missed. Entering a well-stocked library still takes my breath away; books in Africa are rare and either ant- or rat eaten. Providing a steady supply of children's books for our boys was particularly difficult, but we were able to keep them reading through a judicious use of what is available. A teacher at the boarding school, a short plane ride away, allowed us to borrow books from their library. When we learned about the Good Book Club we started receiving regular shipments of books of their choice. A retired librarian in England shipped us the twenty books she thought every young person should read. Later a group of missionaries combined their personal libraries, and started a lending service of their own, and more recently we downloaded the classics and copyright-free books from the internet.

The other thing that still takes my breath away is a visit to a hardware store. We could buy nails once in a while, but only one particular size. I once pointed out to a shopkeeper that two inch nails were available in several stores, but that he was more expensive than his neighbors. "The customers will all come to me when the others have run out of nails," he replied laconically.

The need for simplicity in Africa forces one to be imaginative, and to tackle many jobs that only specialists would do in the West. I once made a new toilet seat from an old packing case. In fact, I even built a whole new bathroom once. Building the septic tank, creating a simple cistern for fresh rain water, and connecting solar panels were a challenge. However, I was rewarded with a tremendous sense of accomplishment while enjoying my first hot shower.

Doing Surgery

Early in my career I dealt with a lot of arrow wounds, but more recently the main problem has been gunshot wounds. Falling from trees once accounted for a considerable amount of trauma, but now it is motorbike accidents. The headmaster of Nyankunde high school had a motorbike accident, as a result of which he ended up with a very stiff right knee. I told him that if he gave me his bike he would avoid additional injuries! If only he had followed my advice... He had a second accident which badly damaged his left knee. For the rest of his life he hobbled around on two stiff knees.

Recent literature for surgeons in the developing world encourages a return to the most simple of techniques. Fortunately, there is also an ever increasing amount of advice available through books, journals, videos and the internet in which considerable thought is given to managing problems without all the sophisticated equipment which seems necessary in the West.

I have kept my surgical techniques as simple as possible, partly because of the paucity of things available, partly to teach appropriate surgery to our Congolese students, and partly to keep costs at a minimum. Although my techniques may be simple and cost-effective, I wholeheartedly believe they can be as good, and at times better, than what is available in the West. Patients may need to spend a longer time in the hospital, and physical examinations may take longer, but the final results are usually excellent. It is, for instance, quite possible to make very fine surgical sutures with a pair of pliers, fishing line and a hypodermic needle—as good as anything that comes readymade out of a surgical packet. Simple surgery does not necessarily mean dangerous surgery. Surgery becomes dangerous when you try and cut corners, or when a surgeon is operating in the middle of the night with inadequate light or inadequate anesthesia. We keep a back-up generator for those times when the power goes off, and we store water in the operating room for those many days when no water comes out of the tap.

There were times when I wished that some of the hospitals in which I have operated were better equipped in either instruments or personnel. However, all you really need are a good autoclave to ensure sterility, and nurses and doctors who understand aseptic techniques. The autoclave can be as simple as a pressure cooker over three stones; the important question is whether the staff know how to use it. I generally operate under a form of local anesthetic so that I can talk to the patient. This helps me to make sure he or she is not suffering unduly, and is breathing easily. I have gotten used to tying many knots with ligatures made from cheap Chinese nylon which we sterilize ourselves, so we don't need an electrical cautery machine.

We try to keep track of infection rates. They vary wildly from one hospital to the next, for the simple reason that some take greater care in handling all the sterile materials in the operating room. The British speak of an "operating theater" because of all the carefully choreographed steps you must take to avoid extraneous bacteria from entering into a wound. To my chagrin I have found teaching these "aseptic techniques" difficult, not least because the contaminating bacteria are, of course, invisible and it is only too easy to brush unwittingly against a non-sterile surface. Almost every newly graduated doctor will break the basic rules of surgery and cause a post-operative infection.

The problem with more complicated instruments, like incubators, cautery, endoscopy, ultrasound, even computers, is twofold: the word for "maintenance" does not exist in Swahili and, secondly, constant variations in voltage plays havoc with sensitive electronics. Third-world hospitals are storehouses of non-functioning equipment in need of an engineer with both ability and imagination.

One of the most common operations I do are prostatectomies. In fact, my first surgical rotation as a medical student at Barts Hospital in London was with a Dr. Badenoch, who had removed the prostate of a prime minister, a chief of staff and, no doubt, various other important British dignitaries. I have adopted and adapted his technique. The reason I ended up doing this operation so often may have had something to do with the disinclination of others to attempt it because of the possibility of post-operative bleeding. There is always some bleeding, and it needs good nursing care to avoid complications, but almost invariably the patients do well. Hernias and Cesareans are the stock-in-trade for most of our new young surgeons. Sadly, we also receive a regular stream of patients from failed operations elsewhere, where a poor understanding of the anatomy, poor lighting or insufficient anesthesia led to complications, usually damaged guts and bladders.

While it is a luxury to operate on a goiter under general anesthesia with an anesthetist, this is not possible in many outlying hospitals. It is amazing how a huge goiter can be removed using only local anesthesia after a heavy premedication sedative.

There are endless opportunities for those who want to do research. Many diseases common in Africa are rare elsewhere. For instance, we have no idea why we see so many tumors of the lower jaw. These are by no means all the same; many different pathologies can be recognized. Nor is there standardization with regard to age. It was Dr. Dennis Burkitt, working in Kampala, who recognized a lymphoma of the lower jaw in children to be a specific entity now called Burkitts Lymphoma. He went on to show that the disease is almost exclusively found in the malarial belt across Africa, and then showed that it was a viral illness transmitted by the mosquito. Burkitts Lymphoma is a fascinating disease because it is one of the rare cancers that responds remarkably well to anti-cancer drugs; you will see marked improvement after just one week of treatment. Unfortunately if patients stop the treatment too soon it is likely to recur elsewhere in the body, often in the abdomen.

I once removed a huge jaw tumor from a young man from Mulita, a small village 350km from any well equipped and staffed operating room. I knew I could not operate on him there, for local anesthesia was not appropriate and I could not ensure an airway during a complicated surgery. I told him he would need to come to our hospital more than 1000km away. He was given the money to come on a missionary plane, and he was delighted and most grateful with the result of his surgery. His hugely disfigured face was restored, and he is now on the look-out for a wife. Patients in Congo are very appreciative of the fact that we can offer good care for the majority of their illnesses at a fraction of what it would cost elsewhere.

All of our nursing college students need to undertake a research project. Often this consists of nothing more than calculating the frequency of a particular illness, but sometimes some interesting results turn up. One student was able to show that 19 of 20 water sources that he tested were contaminated with coliform bacteria. All this to say that simple living need not involve a lowering of standards; it involves using the gifts, abilities and experience the Lord has given us in a more efficient way.

Working in the emergency department of busy western hospitals can be heartbreaking. I have witnessed large numbers of suicide attempts. The desire to end one's life is often precipitated by an absence of meaning in life; the void becomes so painful that death is perceived as preferable. It is a mystery to my African friends why westerners want to kill themselves when they are phenomenally rich compared to the rest of the world. Suicide is very rare in Africa; I can only remember one case where a young man hung himself from a tree, and this was considered a major catastrophe for the village where it happened. Incredulity was mixed with shame that such a thing had taken place. According to an ancient custom the tree the youth had used had to be chopped down, completely burned—including the stump and root—in order to remove any possible consequence.

Teaching

One of our priorities in Congo has been educating young Africans. When we first arrived at Nyankunde I assumed that I would be a full time surgeon and Nancy would take over as head of the nursing school from Dr Helen Roseveare. However, Africa is still very much a man's world, as a result of which I was appointed head of the school. Helen had had a hard time in her last few years in Congo. Her second year students had been quite a handful, and we had them for their last year. They did not make our first year in Congo easy. I recently met a student from that year. He has since become the lead pastor of a church in Niania. At first he did not recognize me and I did not recognize him—he found out who I was by asking others who the white man was (clearly, time has not been kind to me!). However, he thanked me most sincerely for the training he had had, but I don't think he ever understood how difficult he had made life for us. He also gave me an update on some of the rest of the class; some have passed into glory, but many are still working in medicine.

One course I taught involved teaching simple mathematics in order to calculate drug dosages. Rather than teach a classic course, I created a "mathematics laboratory" where students had to weigh some dried foods and calculate how much was needed for, say, a 10 kg child who needed 3 grams of protein a day. Another exercise involved measuring the circumference of catheters and calculating their (French) gauge. The course I enjoyed teaching most was Community Health. We would select some local village, map it, and then go there every week to measure different indicators of the health of the population. We would discuss our results with the village elders and decide with them how to proceed.

I also tried to encourage the students to use our small library. I would give three students a week, a book which they had to read, after which they had to give an oral book report to their classmates. For many this was the first time they had read through a whole book. The book they enjoyed most was a detective story written for students of French, as it had a very simple vocabulary.

Learning the students' names was a challenge. Initially we only took 25 students in every class so learning their names was manageable. Then, when President Mobutu banned "Christian" names in his push for "authenticity", their names began to sound very complicated to these Western ears. The alphabetical list of our first year class that year began as follows: Adrabho, Adukule, Bakyoghomu, Bokolombong... Today I have over 120 students in the classes I teach, and I have given up trying to remember their names.

Committee meetings took place in the early evenings, as did soccer practice. Although we had a poor basketball court which was also used for volleyball, it was soccer that everyone was passionate about. All that was needed was a ball, but even that could be difficult to find. Chinese balls, though cheap even in the heart of the Congo, seem to be made from some type of heavy paper and disintegrate when wet. However, the students always managed to find one, and as their skill increased they eventually obtained uniforms and even proper soccer shoes. They called their team 'Molunge', which means 'sweat' in Lingala. One year they made it to the quarter finals of the provincial championship.

We tried to organize a social event on Saturday evenings. This might consist of a 'Soiree Musicale'. With little or no warning the students would form some marvelous a cappella groups and solos. Helen had obtained a 16mm film projector from somewhere. After dark we'd project a film on a large bed sheet hanging outside. You could watch the movie from either side of the sheet.

The students at Nyankunde are housed in two dormitories, one for the guys and the other for the girls; keeping the guys from the girls was always a problem. Rooms are simple; each student has a small locker and a bunk bed. We started off with proper flush toilets with a septic tank, but as the hospital grew and the demands on our simple water system increased, we had to provide pit toilets outside.

Amazingly, in the early 1970's we obtained considerable financial support from the central government in Kinshasa. The teachers all received a small salary; expatriate missionary teachers like ourselves would donate theirs to the school's building fund as we were supported by churches and friends outside the country. The students would receive 2 Zaires a month, about $4. Since we provided room and board this was pocket money for them. All money was channeled through the church coordination office since the church was the school's official owner. Because of these financial arrangements we could keep classes small and offer them good supervision and good practical experience. As mentioned earlier, we had an annual intake of 25 new students, which meant that usually some 20 students would graduate from the four year program. Today the school receives no support whatsoever from the government, and there are hardly any missionaries left. This means that today the nursing college takes in 130 students each year so that academic fees can cover expenses. As a result grading papers has become a huge chore, and finding well-supervised places for practical internships is either difficult or impossible.

The church medical center also made education a priority. We have trained people in accounting, organized continuing education seminars, tried to place Christians whom we have known for some time into positions that handle money, and we have tried to put good accountability systems into place. Even so we've had to discharge people because large sums of money went missing. People trained in accounting are hard to find, so even if they are dismissed for irregularities they easily find another job, usually with a government agency where they do not seem to notice—or mind—that every so often money goes missing.

Jesus said, "So if you have not been trustworthy in handling worldly wealth, who will trust you with true riches? And if you have not been trustworthy with someone else's property, who will give you property of your own?" (Luke 16:11-12)

The African Church

The church in Africa is not only growing, it is an exciting place to worship God. Many churches are full on Sundays, and there are usually multiple services. Worship is spirited for the Congolese are very musical. Choirs singing hymns and choruses dance with the music, and the congregation is encouraged to move in time with the music. Cantor singing, in which a leader sings a line which the congregations then repeats was first used in political rallies, but has now been adopted by the church. This system works well in a country where many people are still illiterate and where books are in short supply.

There are, however, also major problems in the church, particularly when it has been given large sums of outside funds to administer. Thankfully, little money has disappeared in the churches our mission organization has helped establish. On the other hand, they always struggle to find enough money for their many projects—something which has forced them to keep their eyes on the Lord and pray hard. Admirably, the main French speaking church in Bunia has launched and accomplished a big building program, but decided to do so without outside help. Some of their own people have really given sacrificially.

Money: Africa's Insecure Commodity

Money in Africa is a very insecure commodity. It is produced by the government, which gives it its value. In 1985 the government of Congo (then Zaire) decided to change the color of its banknotes. All the old, blue five-Zaire notes were declared valueless on December 25. The banks would only honor the new, green five-Zaire notes. At the same time, previously green ten-Zaire notes were changed to new blue ones. Although in theory people could exchange their old money for the new until the end of the year, only a single bank could supply the four million people living in the north-east of Congo. Furthermore, they printed very few new notes, so only a very few people were able to change their savings. Soon bundles of the old, now useless currency were kicked around the streets like footballs.

This sudden demoneterization had a marvelous effect on increasing the value of the new currency on the foreign exchange, even though countless numbers of formerly wealthy people were devastated financially. By and large the Congolese population took this bad news in their stride, as they do all other bad news of fighting, war and corruption. In the entire country only a single bank was burnt to the ground, and we heard reports of three suicides. In general this peaceable nation accepted with little complaint the lot their dictator cast them. The Zairian government had every legal right to do what they did, even if morally they were bound to respect the value of the notes they themselves had issued. In any case, we have no guarantee that in a time of crisis other governments might not resort to the same strategy.

Excursion 6: "The Love of Money"

"No servant can serve two masters: for either he will hate the one, and love the other; or else he will hold to the one, and despise the other. You cannot serve both God and mammon" (Luke 16:13).

Luke chose not to translate the Aramaic word "mammon" which Jesus used when referring to money. As a result neither Tyndale nor the translators of the King James Version of the Bible translated it either. It is generally agreed, however, that "mammon", could be translated as the word "money". In fact, Luke seems to refer more to the use made of money than to money itself. He prefaces the word with the adjective "unrighteous" (Luke 19:9 RSV) The New International Version expresses the concept of "unrighteous mammon" as "worldly wealth". We can think of it as money used for purely selfish purposes.

Luke went on to describe Jesus' meeting with a rich young ruler, and the enormous challenge Jesus put before him (Luke 18:18). This story greatly challenged C.T. Studd, the founder of WEC International. He too came from a wealthy family and, when serving as a missionary in China, learned that he had inherited a fortune. Although the British Consul in Shanghai strongly advised him to hang on to a significant proportion, he determined to do that which the young rich young ruler could not bring himself to do: to give it away. He ended up giving it to the Salvation Army, the China Inland Mission and other organizations. He kept just a small sum for his wife, in the event he should ever marry. When he eventually did marry his wife scolded him for not giving away everything—and saw to it that the rest of the money was given away as well.

Although putting this passage into practice did not seem to trouble C.T. and his wife, it does trouble most of the rest of us. It seems too radical, too abrupt, too thoughtless. Also, various religious charlatans have used it to finance their own "ministries". Still, there is a truth here which "moderation" can easily overlook. Luke places the story in a section of his gospel that deals with the cost and character of discipleship. The question this "man of great wealth" (Luke 18:23) posed Jesus ("Good teacher, what must I do to inherit eternal life?") indicates that he sensed that his spiritual life was inadequate. He wanted to go deeper. However, he seemed to believe that eternal life was something one could earn, or merit, by what one does: "What must I do?"

As he often did, Jesus responded with a question of his own: "Why did you call me good?", which he followed up with some teaching. First of all, the young man would not understand anything about Jesus until he grasped that our standards of goodness are utterly different from God's absolute goodness and righteousness: "Only God is good". Then he pointed the young man to God's basic moral/ethical standard, the Ten Commandments. The young man assured Jesus that he had kept them all since he was a boy. No sooner had he made this statement, however, when Jesus delivers his punch line: "Sell everything you have and give to the poor and you will have treasure in heaven. Then follow me." This was too much for the man. He could not do it.

Many a wealthy person has tried to buy their way into God's good graces by funding the construction of cathedrals, temples, and mosques. If they gave enough, they would be remembered as a benefactor by having their names inscribed on a wall or stained glass window. Jesus, however, does not suggest anything as "practical" or "beautiful" as a great place of worship. "Sell your property and give the proceeds to those least able to reciprocate..."

Paul states that "The love of money is a root of all kinds of evil" (1 Timothy 6:10). The love of money often supersedes our love of God. As Jesus said earlier 'No servant can serve two masters. Either he will hate the one and love the other, or he will be devoted to the one and despise the other. You cannot serve both God and Money" (Luke 16:13). The truth of the matter is that money has a way of polluting us. It tempts us to compromise our values in order to gain and retain it. Money tempts us to do that which is wrong, or unethical, or self-serving—behavior we then rationalize with the idea that we are "just being good stewards". If we fear the loss of our money—whether as a result of charitable giving or as a result of a stock market crash—then we are not fully surrendered to Jesus. Listen to what he has to say on the subject:

"If anyone comes to me and does not hate his father and mother, his wife and children, his brothers and sisters—yes, even his own life—he cannot be my disciple. And anyone who does not carry his cross and follow me cannot be my disciple" (Luke 14:26-27).

"In the same way, any of you who does not give up everything he has cannot be my disciple" (Luke 14:33).

"For whoever wants to save his life will lose it, but whoever loses his life for me will save it" (Luke 9:24).

"Whoever tries to keep his life will lose it, and whoever loses his life will preserve it" (Luke 17:33).

Jesus followed up his challenge with a wonderful invitation: "Come, follow me!" (18:22b). He also invites us to come and follow him on a spiritual journey in which we can enjoy his presence, be taught by his Word and Spirit, experience His provision for all we need for His service, become part of his great extended family—His global body—and be filled with hope during the closing days of our journey as we rest in his promises and feel his comfort.

The rich young ruler, though sincerely seeking the best way forward, found the price too high. Sadly he turned from Jesus and the disciples, for he had broken the first commandment, "You shall have no other gods before me" (Exodus 20:3). In the process there was something else he broke: Jesus' heart. Jesus was sad to see him go. Some of us might have been tempted to lower the entry requirements in order to get him to join our company of disciples, but Jesus refused to lower his high standards. "How hard it is for the rich to enter the kingdom of God," Jesus said, looking at him. "It is easier for a camel to go through the eye of a needle than for a rich man to enter the kingdom of God." Rare indeed is the rich man who will be saved.

Jesus gently calls us as well: "Come, follow me". The challenge is there: complete surrender to Him, and the demolition of any and all hindrances that prevent us from wholeheartedly doing so.

7

Liberian Labor

WE LEFT CONGO to live in Liberia for two years, largely as a result of our boys' educational needs. Neither one wanted to go to boarding school, and we didn't want to send them away. There was a need for two doctors at ELWA[6], where they had recently opened up the West Africa Christian High School. We thought we would be there for the next 10 years at least.

After fourteen years in Congo we considered ourselves hardened missionaries, and told the mission we could do without air conditioned accommodation. They gave us a fully air conditioned house in which to live—and were we ever grateful for the privilege! In 100% humidity and temperatures often in the 90s Fahrenheit we could get the temperature down to 80 degrees. We ran the dehumidifier all the time.

We lived in a beautiful location. Someone once asked our son Tim how close he lived to the sea. "We are twelve palm trees from the beach," he replied. The place was a schoolboys' heaven. School started at 7.30 AM and finished at 1 PM, so every afternoon they were out playing with their friends. We often wandered along the beach as a family when the sun set and the temperature dropped. Locals would be launching small boats, braving the huge breakers, heading out for a night of fishing. To the west of us, towards Monrovia, the capital, was a small village with several ancient canons lying half buried in the sand; at one time it was a shipping point for the slave trade.

Saturday afternoons on the beach were an expatriate social event. Liberians rarely swam; swimming was not safe along much of the coast because the heavy undertow could drag you far out to sea, and because of

---

[6] ELWA is the call sign assigned to a large radio station on the site of an international church hospital and school.

the sharks. However the beach near ELWA had a rocky breakwater within which it was safe to swim. Small tropical fish, anemones and other sea life made the place a snorklers' delight.

For me, however, the years at ELWA were not easy, partly because I was on call every other night and every other weekend—unless my colleague was away, at which time I was on call all the time! It was exhausting. As a result of its past link with the United States, Liberia had adopted an American form of medical practice which made it more difficult to delegate tasks within the medical team than had been the case in Congo. For instance, in Liberia all lumbar punctures had to be done by a doctor, while in Congo the head nurse in pediatrics would do the procedure two or three times a day. Furthermore, the hospital in Liberia was not a teaching hospital so there appeared to be much less of an interest to learn, and much less incentive for people to develop in their medical skills. As a nurse once told me, "I am a nurse, you are a doctor-let me get on with my work, you get on with yours."

Amazingly, we did almost the same amount of daily surgery as we had at Nyankunde, but with less than a quarter the number of beds. In other words, we did much more day surgery and did many surgeries under local anesthesia.

I did do some teaching at the Monrovia School of Medicine, but it was all classroom stuff, the sort of things you can learn from a book. Conspicuously absent was laboratory work and the practical teaching that encourages initiative and the application of theory. As elsewhere in university work in Africa, the opportunity to pass on my experience in surgery and diagnostic skills was limited, to say the least. Still, after being on the edge of nowhere in Congo, it was wonderful to be able to enjoy the delights of a major city, including a selection of restaurants to choose from, as well as a number of supermarkets for your weekly shopping—you could even get ice cream.

We also got to know some people working at the British embassy. The embassy building was a large colonial house in a delightful setting out on Mamba Point, next to the sprawling American Embassy compound. Because there was no Canadian embassy, the Brits looked after us. We would be invited to the Commonwealth Day dinner, at which all other guests would be ambassadors from various African countries. Nancy once sat next to the Nigerian ambassador, and wondered what they would have to talk about. She had the good sense to ask about his family, and spent the rest of the dinner listening to him tell how he had left one member after another in the various countries in which he had served as ambassador. He had a daughter studying in New York, and a son at a university in Moscow.

Once an ambassador came to our hospital with a severe nose bleed. Afterwards we were invited to the Moroccan Embassy for a garden party, to celebrate the 14th anniversary of the accession of King Hassan. It was a beautiful evening. As we signed the guest book, to be forwarded to the king, the Master of Ceremonies, reading over our shoulders, announced our names over a loud speaker system. A reception at the Guinean embassy was a more somber affair. Our two boys were the only children present and, thankfully, were on their best behavior that night. More than one dignitary commented that they would not have dared bring their own children.

Christmas 1989 was particularly memorable. Some dear friends, Hans and Margrit Rothenberger and their 3 children, came to visit us from Cote d'Ivoire (Ivory Coast). We were joined by another Swiss couple, their 3 children and his parents, so we had a great Christmas meal on picnic tables on the beach. However, vague reports of troubles from the north were filtering through, so the Rothenbergers quickly drove up the one highway back to Cote d'Ivoire. The roads were strangely empty. Clearly, something was going on somewhere. However, they reached home without incident. It turned out that Charles Taylor had started his invasion in the north of the country to oust Samuel Doe as President.

Samuel Doe had seized power some 10 years earlier by assassinating the then president, Charles Talbot, in the Presidential Palace. At the time he was just a sergeant in the Liberian army. When his commanding officer arrived at the palace to proclaim himself president, Samuel Doe said (or so the story goes), "No, you are not the president, I am." Until Doe's coup Liberia had been ruled by the descendants of the freed American slaves who had founded the country in 1834. This ruling elite had more or less made slaves of the local Liberians. Doe was the first (and to this day the last) local Liberian to become president.

Doe was not popular. He was not a particularly literate man and his financial policies were disastrous. The country had used the American dollar for many years, but now began issuing its own Liberian Dollars, Doe Dollars, whose value only ever fell. As things deteriorated we noticed a Boeing 707 flying slowly above Monrovia painted in the presidential colours. Presumably it was part of Doe's exit strategy.

Although he himself was poorly educated, Doe did seem to value learning, and it was rumored that he might leave office if he was offered a suitable scholarship. I even wrote to Emmanuel College in Cambridge, suggesting they should offer him a position in a Cambridge PhD program. I don't think anyone took me seriously as I got no reply. Cambridge might not have done well out of the offer, but many people in Liberia might still be alive today, and Monrovia might still have some of the infrastructure destroyed during the war, and still not rebuilt.

News was scarce during the war. The national radio station only made light of the situation. Fighting was obviously going on up in the north, but it was difficult to know exactly what the situation was like. "The army is continuing its mopping up operations," was about all we heard from the national station. The most accurate news came to us via the BBC World Service, which was rebroadcast on ELWA radio several times a day. Then, in April, the government prohibited the station from re-broadcasting these news bulletins.

The great advantage of democracy is that it provides a way to get rid of bad leaders. Having come to power by force, however, it seems that the only way to depose this president was by force. Charles Taylor and his "rebels" surprised us all. There is only one decent road running north to south through the country, the two-lane, paved road from Monrovia to Gban. There is also an unpaved track running parallel to this main road, some 50 km to the east. It runs down to Buchannan on the coast, a town just 20 kilometers or so to the east of Robertsfield, the main international airport. On this road some 20 km. north of Buchanon, at a place called Gaypeter, there was a small WEC church. Once a week an Australian missionary lady in Monrovia, Denise White, had radio contact with its pastor, Rev. Louis Mumford. "How are things Pastor?"

"Oh, just fine. Things are quite quiet here since the rebels have come." That was the first indication that Charles had taken the minor road south, and was now just some 50 km from the main airport. Denise quickly contacted the British embassy, who also looked after the Australians. We were visited by the local warden from the British embassy the next day. "The ambassador thinks that you should leave the country now while there are still commercial flights in and out of Monrovia. We think there will be heavy fighting for the capital." We immediately went over to our American boss to ask his permission to book a flight. Much to our surprise, he was not at all sympathetic. "We don't take too much notice of what the British Embassy says. We will wait to hear what advice the Americans give. If we need to evacuate, the US will lay on special planes."

"If there is a US-led evacuation, will they take everyone?"

"Well... they will take Americans first."

I had received an invitation to attend a WEC leaders' meeting in Scotland, and when we mentioned this, our boss reluctantly consented. "You could tell everyone you are going early to attend a conference. I don't want you upsetting the rest of the team and giving them ideas about leaving." We booked a ticket with British Airways for Thursday, May 14, and were surprised to learn that the airline could still offer us an "air locker" for as much baggage as we wanted—we just needed to pay for the extra weight we put in it. We had regretted leaving our library in Congo, so decided that this time we would take most of our books and many of the boy's toys. That turned out to be the last BA flight out of Robertsfield for several years. As we were leaving for the airport we learned that the Americans had ordered a general evacuation. Special planes would be available in two days' time, on the Saturday: "All expatriates should leave. We are laying on special flights and no one can take more than 20kg of personal baggage."

We were informed that our BA flight was 40% overbooked, so were on tenterhooks to know if we would get on it or not. People were going around the departure lounge offering to change Liberian dollars at a very poor exchange rate, and generally trying to make off with what the forced evacuees had to leave behind. As it was, our plane had several spare seats in the back. Apparently some people had booked several flights, and were waiting to see how the situation panned out before they headed for the airport.

Not everyone left the hospital. Two brave doctors stayed to keep the hospital open. They were initially well received by Charles Taylor's troops, who took over the ELWA radio station to broadcast his demands to the president. This provoked heavy artillery fire which eventually obliterated the station. Our two doctors were at the mercy of whomever in this lawless conflict wished to profit from them. They were robbed of everything they had, including their wedding rings. In the end they were forced to walk in their underwear some 12 km along the beach to the American Embassy, from where they were eventually taken out by helicopter.

Charles Taylor and his troops got within 100 meters of the presidential palace before a UN brokered cease fire was put in place. During this stalemate anarchy reigned. There was no meaningful government for many months, until after the elections, which Taylor won. One cannot help but wonder if there would have been far less suffering if Taylor had been allowed to take the presidency by force. One of many people who suffered immensely during this power vacuum was the hapless President Doe. He was arrested while attending a peace conference of the major rebel leaders, after which he was slowly executed. A video circulating among Americo-Liberians showed him having his fingers cut off one after the other.

A year later I returned to the ELWA hospital to help Dr. Steve Befus reopen it. The only way in was via a small UN plane from Freetown, Sierra Leone, to the small Spriggs Paine airport in the middle of Monrovia. Seeing the wanton destruction everywhere was heartbreaking. Many roads were blocked with disabled cars pushed end to end to prevent the advance of troops. None of the hospital's many houses were habitable; we stayed off campus in an isolated house which the mission used to rent. The hospital grounds were covered with shell cases. At one time the hospital was home to several thousands of displaced people from Monrovia who had had nothing to eat except 'palm hearts', so all the palm trees along the shoreline had been cut down for food. Our morgue was full of decomposing bodies. We got a digger to excavate a hole and buried them.

I took out an autoclave and, once more, surgical supplies were sterilized over 3 stones and a wood fire. It was back to the basics—but we were operating again. Today the hospital is once again offering good service to the people of Liberia.

Excursion 7: "Laying Up Treasures in Heaven"

"Do not be afraid, little flock, for your Father has been pleased to give you the kingdom. Sell your possessions and give to the poor. Provide purses for yourselves that will not wear out, a treasure in heaven that will not be exhausted, where no thief comes near and no moth destroys. For where your treasure is, there your heart will also be" (Luke 12:32-34).

When you are caught up in a war and your life is in danger you soon learn that there are more important things to worry about than money. However, as already stated, we cannot live in most places in the world without money. Jesus tells us to keep track of that which we have been given: "To him that has will more be given, but to him that has not even that which he has will be taken from him" (Luke 19:26). This is a general principle in business: if you invest in something you expect a return. We are stewards of the resources given to us.

The biblical story is one of stewardship. From the garden of Eden, which God entrusted to Adam, to the gospel, which He entrusts to us, God holds people accountable for the gifts He gives them. When He gave Israel land, it came with instructions on how it should be divided and who should manage each portion. Similarly, when He entrusts the gift and responsibility of children to parents, and the care of a congregation of Christians to pastors, we are to "guard what has been entrusted to your care" (2 Timothy 1:14). Stewardship means that the object in our trust does not, in fact, belong to us. Stewards are expected to administer the property of another, responsibly. They are to be careful guardians of that which has been entrusted to them. For instance, parents do not, ultimately, "own" their children, but they are responsible to love, nurture and raise them so that they become valuable adult members of society.

Thankfully, we are not left to our own devices in this task of stewardship. God has given numerous guiding principles to help His stewards carry out their task wisely. One of these principles is generosity. The realization of the importance of generosity is, I believe, a God-given insight.

Obviously, the power which comes with money can be used for good or evil. If there is no underlying ethical framework to control and limit its acquisition it can easily be misused. Sadly, accountability systems are usually needed to keep us honest; if no one ever checks up on us it is all too easy to fall into bad practices. In Jesus' famous parable of the shrewd manager (Luke 16:1-9), the money he used so generously to earn people's favour was not his own, it belonged to his boss. In the same way, "our" money does not, ultimately, belong to us; it is a gift from God sanctioned by the State. We are called to be generous and to use it for eternal purposes. Using it to improve relationships with others should be our aim. We have to choose between using it on people or on things-for-self. In the end, we will be called to give an account of our stewardship.

Jesus taught that money should be used for the good of others through acts of charity. These can then become stepping stones to more permanent benefits as we invest in relationships or friendships. According to Jesus, spending money in this way can lead to deeper fellowship with God, as well as with the people we could help who, on the Day of Judgment, will testify to our unselfish use of money. This other-worldly investment of money is how we can generate "true wealth."

"Laying up treasure in heaven" is a very different process from laying it up here on earth. According to Jesus, it begins with the sale of one's possessions in order to give to the poor. As we have seen, this was his advice to the rich ruler in Luke 18. In Luke 12, in the passage mentioned above, Jesus is talking to His disciples as a group. Basically, he tells them not to be afraid of his radical teachings on the subject of money.

Treasure in heaven has more to do with "being" than "owning". It involves a richness of life focused on friends, occupations and relationships, rather than on the possession of money. It is all about happiness, security and lasting peace of mind rather than a healthy bank balance. We might call it "long-lasting wealth" or, perhaps better, "true wealth".

We noted that money represents power which can be used for good or evil. When used for good it is converted into something better. It generates "true wealth" which satisfies by rewarding those who possess it with peace and security. Earthly wealth leaves one with that "I could use a second helping" feeling. It is only useful for the duration of this life; true wealth is of eternal value. Earthly wealth has no value in and of itself, as we discovered when the Congolese currency became worthless. True wealth, on the other hand, includes family, friends, and a bright future. Earthly wealth decreases in value; true wealth always keeps its value.

The bottom line is that one's use of money comes down to a single choice: according to Jesus is is impossible to ardently pursue both money and God. It is either the one or the other. A sermon which John Wesley often preached was based on Luke 12:33: "Lay not up for yourselves treasures upon earth..." According to Wesley Christians should give away all but the bare necessities of life, i.e., plain wholesome food, clean clothes and enough to carry on one's business. One should earn what one can, justly and honestly. Capital need not be given away, but all income should be given to the poor after bare necessities are met. Wesley lived what he preached. He always wore inexpensive clothes and dined on simple food. He eschewed wearing a wig, the custom at the time, in order to save money. Sales of his books earned him up to 1,400 Pounds Sterling annually, but on average he spent about 30 Pounds a year on himself. He gave the rest away. "If I leave behind me 10 Pounds," he once wrote "you and all mankind bear witness against me that I lived and died a thief and a robber."

8

Canadian interlude

BEFORE THE civil war in Liberia had erupted we had been approached about returning to Canada to become the leaders of WEC's Canada branch. Our return to Canada and adaptation to life in North America proved to be one of the most difficult times we experienced as a family, and also one of our most difficult times financially. It seems that some of our supporters felt that it was a waste for two well-trained doctors to leave the medical profession to drum up support for missions.

In the end our support did not drop, but our expenses skyrocketed. We had to furnish a small apartment, purchase suitable clothes, and send our boys to school. The latter was a particularly difficult choice, as well as the most expensive one, as we both felt that we should send them to a private school.

The choice of a school was not taken lightly, and not without looking at various alternatives. In spite of the expense, we opted for a private school, Hillfield Srathallan, where both boys ended up doing well. Jeremie had shown considerable potential and needed to be stretched. Throughout his school years he came second in his class, but won the Pascal prize in mathematics from Waterloo University in his final year in high school. The somewhat more disorganized Timothy responded marvelously to the school's well ordered environment. Although he started as an average student he quickly made the honor roll and was the gold medalist in his last year. Thankfully, the school awarded us a bursary for several years—even though there seemed to have been some consternation on the selection committee: "What are two doctors doing asking for financial help?" Somehow, we convinced them of our need!

We parents can be slow on the uptake. It took us a while to discover that Jeremie needed glasses to see at a distance, a defect which may explain why he became such an avid reader. He loves nothing more than to put his nose into a new book. Nevertheless we felt a bit guilty when, after he received a pair of glasses, we heard him say, "Wow, you could even count the blades of grass if you wanted to!"

It also took us a while to recognize that Tim had a great singing voice and acting ability. When he sung his first solo, "See Amid The Winter's Snow", at a Hillfield Christmas service, I said to Nancy, "that looks like Tim singing!" After that he took many vocal leads, including "Carousel", "Oliver", "Fiddler on the Roof", "My Fair Lady" and "Godspell". This last was an important event in more ways than one: through questions asked by Tim and the cast their English teacher came to faith.

Nancy and I were both appointed to the leadership of WEC Canada. We shared the work, and I was only too happy for her advice after the many interviews we conducted with staff and potential missionary candidates. At the same time, Nancy wanted to update her medical skills. Refresher courses and further training for people in our situation were not easy to find, but eventually a general practice counselor at the College of Physicians and Surgeons of Ontario suggested that Nancy find a general practice physician who would take her under his or her wing and bring her up-to-date with respect to Ontario practices. All she needed now was a willing physician. Through a medical student who had visited us in the Congo she ended up working every Monday in the practice of Dr. Stepita, a general practitioner in Hamilton looking to reduce her practice prior to retirement.

I enjoyed my nine to five type of job. Spending the first hour of every day in prayer and worship with fellow staff members was great, and it was a privilege to work with young, enthusiastic missionary candidates. It was also wonderful to be teaching again, and sharing something of our experience of Africa.

One very special gift from the Lord was our place of residence. Built in 1921, our 14,000 square foot mansion was in one of Hamilton, Ontario's, swankiest areas, close to downtown and just over the road from the city's largest hospital. We were surrounded by doctors working very long hours yet living in much smaller houses. The WEC House is used for orientation courses for missionary candidates and as a rest house for those returning from overseas. There are usually volunteers who come in during the week to help with maintenance, while missionary candidates help with cleaning. For most of that time there was also a cook.

Besides involvement in missionary training and orientation we also organized a number of short term mission trips to various WEC fields. Our first trip was to Brazil with a number of people from our home church in Hamilton, Philpott Memorial. We first helped with general maintenance and the clearance of trees at a Bible College at Minas Gerias, and then went to Bello Horizonte, where we experienced the vibrant work and worship of various newer, evangelical churches. The Baptist church we were associated with had planted some 34 daughter churches!

Next we led a team to Turkey, where we helped distribute Turkish New Testaments. Though perfectly legal (provided the books are printed in Turkey), the police can object to this form of evangelization, meaning that longer term workers there refrain from doing it lest their visas be revoked. Handing out New Testaments is more difficult than it sounds. In our few sentences of atrocious Turkish we tried to communicate that the Quran encourages Muslims to read the 'Torah', the 'Zabur' and the 'Injil', i.e., the Pentateuch, the Psalms and the New Testament. We then tried to say, "This is the Injil". As soon as people heard this they would often refuse to take it—we were only able to distribute a total of 73 copies.

We also took a team to Mexico, where we helped organize two vacation Bible schools. Some of the young people who joined us on this trip were marvelous, dressing up as clowns and thinking up a number of interesting activities to do with the children. Every time we went on a mission trip we took our two boys with us. As they had done in Africa, they could amuse themselves with a minimum of props. Later they became integral members of the team.

Nancy and I also did a lot of travel to various countries for WEC committee meetings designed to make sure that this international organization continued to move forward in unity. During one such trip to Australia we took the opportunity to visit some of our Canadian WEC missionaries in Fiji.

I also traveled extensively across this great country of Canada, mostly to Bible Schools to advertise the need in many parts of the world for help in church work. Canadian Bible School students are a mixed bag: some enroll because they are serious about their Christian lives, others are sent by parents who hope the experience will reform them. In Western Canada, Bible schools typically only run from October to April, during which months it was not possible to do farm work. Bible school enrollment has dropped precipitously, which has pushed these schools down one of two routes: emphasize academics and metamorphose into universities, or emphasize spiritual life and the deeper Christian walk.

WEC's recruitment process is not short. Initial contact is followed by further correspondence, and often personal visits. The organization's best recruiters are its own members who choose to live in one of these Bible schools while they are on home leave. Sadly, many mission organizations are so weak on administration that letters of enquiry often go unanswered.

Sometimes we can't help but nurture doubts about those we send abroad: How will they get on? How about their children? Will they be able to adapt? WEC twice rejected a particular Englishman because of his poor educational background, but the man refused to take 'no' for an answer. WEC finally accepted him—and he now has a PhD in medieval Japanese! One family that we accepted could not get the support of their local church, which felt that their children were too rebellious and would not fit in to an overseas church setting. Once they got to Africa, they sent the oldest boy to a nearby boarding school, and soon the rest of the kids wanted to go there as well. We are still in touch with that oldest son, a delightful fellow.

Not everyone is a success story. We were delighted when the head student from one of the largest Bible Schools joined our ranks, and we used his photograph on one of our recruiting brochures. He went to North Africa, had problems with the team, left for home, and now sells securities in Western Canada.

Different international organizations tackle the challenges of internationalization differently. The most common approach is for different sponsoring countries to take responsibility for different areas of the work. A good example of this model is Medecins Sans Frontiers, where the Swiss office is responsible for Congo, the French office for Cote d'Ivoire, etc. WEC, for its part, has sought to encourage unity among truly international teams working together in all its different fields of service. This helps it avoid cultural imperialism, and gives local Christians a much greater voice in the area of contextualization of the ministry. However, working on such multi-cultural teams does bring its own challenges and stresses.

Early during our time in Canada, WEC decided to open a cross-cultural training centre near Vancouver, British Columbia. My predecessor as director of WEC Canada, who had retired to the Vancouver area, headed up the search for property. The process involved looking at lots of real estate, and engaging in lots of prayer for finance and for guidance. In retrospect we can see how the Lord led us all along and in the end we purchased a church and manse in Abbotsford. An American member of WEC was appointed to head up the training centre. However, we could not get permission to expand the buildings on the site, and our newly appointed director began to get severe doubts about the project. Had we made a mistake?

Then a beautiful but simple boys' home sitting on 5 acres of land came up for sale in Langley, B.C. Asking price 1.5 million dollars, which was way beyond our budget. No sooner had we shown an interest in the property, however, when the British Columbia government revoked the boys' home license; they wanted the boys to be housed with regular families. Suddenly the price dropped to $750,000. We were able to sell the church in Abbotsford for a small profit, and when a number of generous donors also pitched in we completed the purchase. The centre, known as Gateway, has since been adapted and enlarged and offers a number of training and language programs under the direction of Dr. Mike Boling.

Our experience in Africa and elsewhere has convinced me that the world needs missionaries more than ever before. Many countries still have enormous medical, educational and social needs, and the opportunities for Christian doctors, nurses, teachers, agriculturalists and other skilled professionals have never been greater. In my opinion, committed Christians fill these roles better than most others. Missionaries are usually prepared to stay long term and learn the language and culture of those they go to serve. Maybe this is why Matthew Parris wrote a very pithy article in the Times of London entitled, "As an atheist, I truly believe Africa needs God," in which he wrote the following:

"Now a confirmed atheist, I've become convinced of the enormous contribution that Christian evangelism makes in Africa: sharply distinct from the work of secular NGOs, government projects and international aid efforts. These alone will not do. Education and training alone will not do. In Africa Christianity changes people's hearts. It brings a spiritual transformation. The rebirth is real. The change is good."[7]

Obviously, corruption is extremely harmful to the economy of any given country. It may enrich certain individuals or even some companies, but in the long term it is a cancer that starves society of outside investment and help. The Christian gospel, with its clear enunciation of right and wrong and the offer of God's grace to enable us to walk a straight but narrow way is an enormous power for good in the world today. Furthermore, society and churches often need training and other skills that only missionaries can supply. All that to say that we count it a privilege that, for a period of a just over ten years, we could encourage and support the global missionary effort.

Excursion 8: On Persistent Prayer

We cannot live without money in today's world, even though it causes lots of problems. We expect a salary for an honest day's work. The challenge is using the money earned in the best way. And then, what do we do when there are shortages? While in Africa we had enough to cover our living and travel expenses. We even built a house. These things were more difficult in Canada. Here are some financial principles which we sought to put into practice:

1. We look to the one from whom we believe we will receive. Since I work without contract and receive no fixed salary, I will ask God. The principle is based on the fact that He tells us Christians that if we don't ask Him, He won't give. If we determine to live life trusting that He will supply, then we must pray, asking Him for all we need. If, on the other hand, we look to the government or a secular employer to provide our salary, we will ask him or her.

2. We must keep on praying. Like the woman who pestered the corrupt judge (Luke 18), we too should persist in prayer. This parable was about a judge who decided cases in favor of the one who paid the highest bribe. The poor had no hope of justice. Since the poor widow knew she could not out-bribe her opponent, she decided to wear the man down through

---

[7] Parris, M. *As an atheist I truly believe Africa needs God*. Times Online. 7 Jan. 2009

constantly beseeching him. He eventually got so sick and tired of her that he helped her just to be rid of her. Jesus told this story to encourage us to persist in prayer. If a corrupt judge would grant a request, how much more would a loving God answer the request of a widow who had nowhere else to turn? "Will not God bring about justice for his chosen ones, who cry out to him day and night?" Jesus concluded "Will he keep putting them off? I tell you, he will see that they get justice, and quickly."

Why does God want us to persist? Doesn't He hear us the first time? Of course he does! Our persistence shows the intensity of our desire, and our faith that God can supply our need. Persistence in prayer is followed by answered prayer, and results in our faith being strengthened. "Always pray and never give up" (Luke 18: 1).

Persistent prayer should not be confused with unthinking repetition or long-windedness. In Jesus' time there were those who thought God would hear them because of their many words, because of the sophistication of their prayers. (Matthew 6:7). Today there are those who spin prayer wheels and fly prayer flags or kites to stretch out their prayers. Although I do not want to judge these people's motives, it is sad to think that God could describe their efforts as "vain repetitions" (Matthew 6:7). In politics we readily understand the difference between a filibuster and the forceful repetition of a political point close to someone's heart. One is clearly more significant, of more value, than the other.

Each of my two sons has his own unique, very different character. One is a studious introvert, who from an early age could decide exactly what he wanted, and then pursue that with amazing single-mindedness. The other is an extroverted gadfly, who upon our first visit to a large city stared wide-eyed at successive shop windows, his "wants" changing every time something bigger and better captured his attention. The single-minded son received far more of his requests than his sibling, who was forever changing his mind.

3. What is the motive of our prayer? The parable of the Pharisee and the tax collector in Luke 18:9-14 teaches us another principle concerning prayer: it can be used for either selfish or unselfish ends. The Pharisee's prayer was all about himself. Jesus said that he was "confident of his own righteousness and looked down on everybody else." Everything he said about himself may have been true. He may, indeed, have been a very

decent man. But convinced of his own righteousness, he looked down at the despised tax collector. For as long as we look down on others we will not look up to God. Do we approach God in assured self-righteousness, or do we kneel humbly before his throne of grace in great self-awareness of our own sinfulness?

4. What have we done with that which God has already given us? Are we good stewards of what He has entrusted to us? How can we expect God to bless us if we don't use the resources He has already given, wisely and responsibly?

We had a family in our mission with financial problems. Their children were very fond of "tasty taters", a type of frozen, fried potato nuggets. Soon after being made aware of their financial woes I spotted a large bag of fresh potatoes they had been given rotting unused in their garage.

But there is more to it than mere stewardship. Are we being obedient to that which God has called us to? The well-known British evangelist, pastor and writer Alan Redpath once said that he received Christ's second best. He had been called to become a missionary to China, but never went. Although he had a fantastic ministry, it seemed second best to him. All the while he grieved over the fact that he had not obeyed his call to China.

5. Are we generous with what we have, whether that be much or little? Jesus once saw a poor widow put only two cents into the temple treasury, but He commended her for giving a very high proportion of her income (Luke 21:2).

6. Although it is far too simplistic to suggest that unanswered prayer is due to sin, mismanagement or personal failure, that can be the case. Thankfully, God is so much more ready to forgive than we are.

7. Although most of us don't particularly like this fact, the truth is that God can teach us much more through difficulties than when we have all we want. It may be that those shortages have come because He has something particular that he wants to teach us.

8. It may be that "No" is the best answer for us at the moment. We are

human and "see through a glass dimly". Our inability to grasp God's purposes certainly results in disappointments in the short run, but when, eventually, we see the total picture we will, no doubt, be overjoyed that God did not answer particular prayers in the way we thought He should. I do not believe that any prayer is ever unanswered. The answer can be, 'yes', 'no', or 'not yet'. It only appears unanswered when we don't get the answer we expect.

The famous pioneer missionary Hudson Taylor stated that "God's work done in God's way, never lacks God's supply." I suggest that the answer to shortages is prayer, remembering that prayer is a two way process in which we both listen to God as well as talk to Him. We must be prepared to do things God's way, however difficult that may be.

9

Warfare and Wrecking

AFTER GRADUATING from secondary school both our boys left for university, and we felt free to return to Africa. The obvious place to go was back to was Nyankunde, in the country now known as the Democratic Republic of Congo. We knew the languages, and they needed us for teaching and for our medical skills. We'd also received many personal invitations to return. In 2000 we visited the place briefly, and then started making plans to return long term in April 2002.

The north-east of Congo was at war from 1994 to 2005, during which time some 4 million people lost their lives. That conflict has been called "Africa's First World War". In 2000 most of Orientale province was occupied by Uganda, an area as large as Uganda itself. An encampment of Ugandan soldiers near the hospital consisted of simple stick and 'adobe' huts. They were a seedy looking bunch, and because they needed hospitalization so often we reserved a ward for them. Almost all of them suffered from AIDS—which may have been one of the reasons they were drafted for service in Congo. Beside these sick soldiers the struggling population was having great difficulty making ends meet, which made the spread of AIDS even more explosive.

There had been on-and-off fighting around the hospital, but because we treated everybody from all sides, and because many different tribal groups were represented on the staff, we didn't think we would be perceived as taking sides. Furthermore, the hospital was surrounded by a high chain link fence which afforded some protection over our 'neutral' hospital area in the event of trouble. Following the 1918 Geneva Convention on the conduct of war, I had encouraged the administrator to paint some large red crosses on hospital roofs, but this was never done.

Earlier conflicts had taken place when Laurent Kabila passed through in 1996 on his way to Kinshasa, to oust President Mobutu. He had had the support of the Rwandans, who entered central eastern Congo at that time. The Ugandans showed up from the north-east in 1998. Soon after our brief visit in 2000, the local chief of Nyankunde decided that there were too many of the neighboring tribe in the area and not enough of his own tribe, the Bira, and decided to exclude the Giti tribe (a branch of the Lendu) from the area under his control. This made this segment of the population feel very uncomfortable at Nyankunde.They were encouraged to move eastward to Songolo, the nearest large Giti village. The chief was a Bira married to a Hema. All this to say that this event led to major aggravation of the traditional rivalry between Lendu and Hema in the area. The Lendu are short Bantu people who came from the west. They are a largely agrarian, farming community. The Hema, on the other hand, are tall Nilotic people who came from the north and are nomadic cattle herders by tradition. The Lendu complain that the Hema allow cattle to graze on their fields, while the Hema complain that the Lendu are digging fields in their pasture lands.

We knew there was a risk of more fighting, but expected that the hospital would be spared, as it had been in the past. In hindsight we should have taken more notice of what we considered to be very minor incidents. Firstly, our previous cook, Averasi who was Lendu, came to see me in May of 2002. She needed an abdominal operation and wanted me to operate. I was only too happy to oblige, but was most surprised that she wanted to leave the hospital immediately after the operation. Suddenly she came to feel very ill at ease in Nyankunde. Clearly the local situation had become a lot more complex from when we had left it in 1987.

The second incident occurred in August of 2002, when a group of Hema raided the village of Songolo and stole a number of cattle. We watched them returning to Nyankunde proud of having captured these cows from their enemies. In hindsight it is easy to say that we should have cleared out, but we had carefully made our decision to return, and by God's grace, I am still around to tell the story.

Our house had become somewhat dilapidated in our absence, and I was doing some repairs on it. Among other things, we put burglar bars on the windows and reinforced the locks, something which may have saved the life of some in our house when rebels tried to enter it. Nancy had planned to visit Canada for her mothers 90th birthday and, sensing the tension in the air, I encouraged her to leave a few days earlier than originally planned with some young Swiss people who had helped set up a student study center.

The attack came on September 5, 2002. We had had morning prayers as usual at 7 AM, after which I had done my usual ward round visiting my surgical patients. The folks in the operating room told me that they were not yet ready, as there were still items to autoclave. We agreed to start operating at 10 AM, so I went home for a cup of coffee.

The shooting started in the valley at 9 AM on the dot. I could catch a glimpse of numerous Congolese streaming over the hillsides in all directions moving towards the hospital. Just at that moment three women were at the back door trying to sell fruit and vegetables to Marguerite our cook. One of them had a small baby on her back. They all hurried into the house and we locked all the doors and closed all the curtains.

At 11.30 there was heavy knocking at the back door—it sounded as if they might break it down. Fortunately I had repaired the lock only the Saturday before, and it held, though, as I saw afterwards, only barely. I parted the curtains at the kitchen window and saw three heavily armed men in army fatigues with grass in their hair. They were brandishing AK40s, had bullet-belts draped across their chests, and were carrying a rocket propelled grenade. "Open the door," they shouted

"Sorry, I can't let you in," I cried back.

"We'll break the door down!"

"Fine", I replied, "You can break the door down but I can't let you in."

"Give us money."

"We deliberately don't keep money in the house, but I can pray for you!" So I stood in front of the window, closed my eyes, raised my hands and started praying a very long prayer. I can't remember exactly what I prayed for, and I'm sure I did not ask the Lord to bless the activity of these rebels, but I did pray that the Lord's will be done. I also prayed for each of the three individuals banging on the door, even if not for the success of their efforts. They turned away and left before I had finished my prayer, and never came back. The fact that they did not enter the house was a great blessing, as several people would have been killed immediately by virtue of belonging to the Hema tribe.

Essentially what took place was a genocide, tribal warfare style: if you belonged to the wrong tribe you were immediately slaughtered. Several other women joined us in the house that afternoon, and some of our nursing students that evening. There was gunfire all night and into the next morning, but at 10 AM a senior nurse came up to the house wearing a white coat. "We were able to hide a radio. We contacted Mission Aviation Fellowship, and they are sending a plane at midday. If you want to leave you need to go down to the airstrip in your white lab-coat."

"What about all the gunfire we're hearing?"

"We're told this is the militia trying to stop looting in the commercial center of the village."

I made my way to the airstrip passing many dead bodies on the way, some with arrows visible in their bodies. While we waited we were protected by heavily armed rebels, who had set up a machine gun in front of the two aircraft hangers. Gradually our numbers swelled. Dr. Sugimoto, who had been caught in the orthopedic building at 9 AM the previous day and could only now come out joined us, as did Donna Jacobson, the wife of the senior MAF pilot. Her husband had left in the early morning for a day of flying, and she had been left alone with 2 small children. When the rebels broke into her house early in the morning they and numerous other people had paraded through the place demanding money and helping themselves to whatever they fancied. She had hardly slept all night, and was exhausted.

When the plane finally showed up at 2 PM the rebels changed their minds, deciding that they did not want us to leave after all. "We will be moving on to Bunia tomorrow (45km to the east), and don't want you to give the town any warning." A small group of them separated themselves off, and Dr. Toko, the Medical Director, started to negotiate with the same three rebels I had prayed for the day before. After much negotiation they let 21 people leave by plane, but told us not to inform anyone in Bunia about anything. All but one of the missionaries left, along with any African in possession of a passport. A small MAF plane flew me to Bunia, where we were greeted by the region's three unarmed United Nations observers, one each from Egypt, Morocco and South Africa. "What can we do to help?" they inquired politely. One of them ran into Bunia for a bottle of water for us to share. The UN force would later swell to 17,000.

From Bunia we were taken to Entebbe. On the apron of the airport in Uganda someone offered me a mobile phone, and I was able to call the WEC HQ in Canada, where Nancy happened to be eating lunch. I was able to give her a phone number in Uganda where she could reach me. Apparently I also told her that I wasn't sure if we'd ever get back to Nyankunde.

Although it is difficult to give exact numbers, it seems that some 2000 people were killed at Nyankunde that day, including some dear friends, simply because they were Hemas. One student told me he helped bury 638 bodies, mostly by tipping them down pit toilets.

The staff that was left behind tried to keep the hospital running, but no one wanted to go there as people were still losing their lives in and around it. It was a very difficult time for Dr. Toko, the main contact with the rebels. He tried to hide people between the ceiling and roof of the operating room. "We know there are people up there. We have seen you taking food up there. Tell them to come down, we won't harm them." They did come down and were slaughtered immediately, right on the central hospital walkway. After some 10 days, the remaining 150 staff, their families, a Canadian missionary and some remaining patients made the decision to trek through the Ituri forest, one of Africa's most remote areas, to Oicha hospital in the next province, which had not been touched by the war. Within hours they were joined by other displaced people, until their group swelled from 700 to 1700.

It was a struggle to find enough to eat and, particularly, enough to drink in the hot equatorial sun. Every time they reached a stream they descended en masse to drink the water without any attempt at purification. Nevertheless only two people contracted cholera towards the end of the journey, and they managed to recover with medical help. The group had a satellite phone among them, and although the battery weakened rapidly, they were able to get some news of their plight to the outside world. The Daily Telegraph in England published a report, and a United Nations helicopter found them and was able to drop some food. At least 3 babies were born during the two weeks of walking. A wife of one of our Nyankunde nurses went into labor right outside the deserted health center at Idou where, believe it or not, they found a single, untouched sterilized delivery pack which included some baby clothes. The group eventually made it to Oicha without losing anyone.

Nancy arranged for me to be evacuated to the UK, where she eventually rejoined me. We had to decide what to do next. We received invitations from five different African countries in need of doctors, but slowly came to the conviction—in large part through discussions and prayer with the missions committee at Guildford Baptist Church—that we rejoin our colleagues who were now at Oicha. Although the place had been inundated with displaced medical personnel, the Medical Director there responded immediately that, yes, we should come. For the next several months we would establish the university-level nurses' training college in exile, so that our students would experience a minimum of disruption.

On September 5, 2002, we lost everything we owned in Africa: house, furniture, clothes and a large quantity of books we had just bought for the nursing school library. I left with a small bag containing my important documents, a computer and a single change of clothes. Losing virtually everything did not particularly upset me; we'd had a good example in Dr. Roseveare, when she had walked out and left us everything she owned. The Lord had given what we needed for His work in Congo and we were happy to let Him take it back. Many more lost much more than we did—some, including our senior hospital chaplain, gave their lives on that day.

We later met many others who had lost everything they'd owned. Many were quite calm and at peace about it—some, maybe, even a little too fatalistic. Some of the more educated Africans were more deeply touched. One of our former students, now a very competent administrator, came to live with us for a couple of months in Oicha while waiting for his family to join him. He had worked hard outside of his medical job to buy a small truck which he rented out. He'd also started to build a house in Bunia. He too had lost it all, and was severely depressed. Thankfully, he recovered his equilibrium, but no doubt the scars remain.

People have often asked us about the cause of fighting in north-east Congo at that time. I have tried to explain the situation in terms of local tribal rivalries and inter ethnic warfare, but these local differences were manipulated by other players with larger interests. Uganda and Rwanda were both involved. These two reasonably well-administered, small countries with few natural resources, had been eying their mismanaged, huge, asset-rich neighbor to the west. To this day elements from Uganda and Rwanda continue to meddle in Congo affairs and possibly incite tribal differences. Furthermore, multinational mining conglomerates are also known to manipulate the local situation to benefit from the weak and corrupt government of Congo so as to maximize their own profit. Lastly, there is evidence that Colonel Gaddafi of Libya was involved. At least one local chief travelled to his country to seek arms. This may explain why such a large number of Christian mission stations in north-east Congo were targeted in September 2002. Linga and Blukwa were raised to the ground, Bogoro suffered very heavy damage, as did Nyankunde, which was then mined, preventing anyone from living there for a year and a half. All four of these villages once had a large Christian presence.

Excursion 9: "Serving As Sheep Among Wolves"

Luke 10:1-12 teaches that being a missionary is not easy. There is stress, tension, an element of risk, and sometimes great uncertainty. When we returned to the Congo in 2002 we knew that there had been war in the area since 1996, but the hospital had been left untouched, and offered help to whoever needed it from either side of the conflict. More importantly for us, the training programs had continued at Nyankunde. They needed help which we could give.

We may not have realized the full implication of Christ's statement, "Go! I am sending you out like lambs among wolves". As guests invited in by the Congolese government we could not carry weapons and we could not comment on the political situation. We were not even allowed to advise the local chief, nor any Congolese citizen.

When Jesus said, "I am sending you like lambs among wolves", he acknowledged the ferocity of the opposition that true followers of Christ can expect. The image of the lamb refers to the self-sacrificing Pascal lamb slain to redeem people. A follower of Jesus Christ must follow in his footsteps and, as such, can expect the same treatment. The image of the lamb also reminds us that the kingdom of God should be marked by peace and reconciliation. We must confront all attitudes and behavior patterns which do not reflect God's intentions. "Lamb" also suggests that religious commitment cannot be compelled by force. This sets Christianity apart from certain other religions, particularly radical Islam.

When Jesus sent the "sheep", the 72 disciples, he gave them three instructions: in the first place they were bring peace (Luke 10:5), then they were to heal the sick (v. 9) and, lastly, to announce the good news of the kingdom (v. 9).

There are numerous practical details with respect to the carrying out of this task Jesus gives us, which we ignore at our peril. He tells us that being sent out requires letting go of a lot of baggage; we must be able to move quickly, without unnecessary hindrances. There is usually a good deal of excitement and anticipation as we embark on an adventure. Where will the journey lead and how will things turn out? The urge to make a difference is often associated with leaving home and going somewhere else. It seems, somehow, more difficult to make a difference where we have lived and worked for most of our lives.

Our primary message must be that the Kingdom of God has come near you. However, preaching the gospel is more than speaking about it. It's about acting, working as citizens of the Kingdom of God, by bringing peace and healing. Before we start speaking about the kingdom we are to bring peace. Peace here is conceived as a real entity which one is able to give, receive, accept or reject. We need to plan how we might bring the peace and reconciliation of God's kingdom to people, just as much as how we are to explain it to them. Healing is something we need to bring as well. Healing is always needed in war zones. In such situations one realizes more than ever that God is the one who heals: I operate on two different people, one of whom heals beautifully and the other has one complication after another. Like those sheep among wolves, we often feel so powerless!

The work is best done in pairs. Jesus sent the 72 "ahead of him, two by two". Bringing peace, healing and preaching the news of the kingdom is difficult, if not impossible, all by yourself. You will only be effective as you work with other, like-minded people. This, for me, has primarily been my wife, but it has also been good to be part of a larger team. During our early years our team was composed for the most part of fellow missionaries, but in the course of time we have seen more and more nationals take positions of leadership. Eventually we became part of a national team which was completely under national leadership. That has been—for the most part—a very satisfying experience. The person who seeks to make a difference in people's lives by seeking to bring peace, healing and good news, has to check out their plans with others. This is a very important reason why Jesus sent his disciples out in pairs.

Harassment by the wolves of Congo begins with the immigration officials who want to ensure that you never forget who is in charge. It continues with the ongoing harassment and demands for pay at road blocks, for permissions, for a departure tax, etc. etc. Sometimes the wolves eat the lambs, although this has been very rare in Congo. One missionary had to leave when a prayer letter of his which criticized the central government was intercepted. In many other countries, however, Christians lose their lives simply because they are followers of Jesus Christ. Just as he laid down his life for his friends, some of his disciples have had to pay the same price.

When the war started at Nyankunde on the 5th September I felt totally defenceless—it was a time when I had to be totally dependent on Christ. I wondered if I would see Nancy again. However, Christ gave me peace, and I was ready to lay down my life if He wanted me to. Rest assured that through violence, war, crime and famine, God is there with us, his children. The only way we can escape our problem-filled world is through the peace which Jesus Christ offers, a peace which is far beyond the understanding of the world. We are to proclaim that peace, which is nothing more that the arrival of God's kingdom as ushered in by Jesus Christ.

Maybe we all need to prepare for persecution. Christ foretold troubles, not only so that they do not take us by surprise, but that they might confirm our faith! Yes, I now thank God for protecting me, but I thank Him even more for the peace he gave me during that crisis.

10

Rebuilding

THE HOSPITAL at Nyankunde was demolished. We had to start again from scratch. First we rejoined the hospital staff who had walked to Oicha. Dr. Kambale, the Medical Director at Oicha, was a friend we had know since the 1970s when he had lived with us during his time as a medical student at Nyankunde. Back then he always brought the Larousse Medicale or some other book to the dinner table to quiz us on medical subjects while we quizzed him about cultural issues. When he announced that he was thinking of marriage, we told him we would have to vet his fiancée! The delightful Nara courageously spent three weeks with "whites" she had never met before, and we immediately gave them our blessing.

This time we were their guests. They moved refugees out of their guest room so that we could join them. After several weeks they let us have a small baked-brick house on the hospital property. It would be our home for the next 4 years. The hospital complex was served with piped water from a natural spring. We were able to build a warm water system for the bathroom from an old oil barrel under which we could light a wood fire. The hospital generator provided us with electricity from 9 to 12:30 every morning and from 6 to 9 in the evening, just enough to keep a fridge and freezer cold if we did not open them when the electricity was out.

Fortunately Oicha was in the middle of a building program, including a huge, as yet unfinished ward in which they were able to house some of those who had walked from Nyankunde. That building was renamed the Titanic: two-bed cubicles housed one, and sometimes two, complete families. The other site set aside for displaced people was half of the 2 km airstrip which ran through part of town. Once people had put up a simple stick framework, one of the aid agencies that were beginning to arrive would give them a tarpaulin to put over the frame. That way people managed to build reasonably watertight, small, single-room shacks which initially two or three families would share. Some tarps were donated by the United Nations, others by Samaritan's Purse. The strip of land set aside for the refugees was about 50 meters wide, with simple pit toilets along the outer edge.

Water was the next problem. Although there were natural springs and simple wells which the locals used, these were soon overwhelmed by the outsiders. Arrangements were made and soon large, latex bladders were filled daily with fresh water for the refugees.

The next priority was food. There was an abundance of it at the local market, but costs soon started rising—even though very few of the displaced had any savings. However prices stabilized when local farmers realized they could sell more food locally without having to bother with transport costs to the south, where most of their produce normally went. The U.N. World Food Program also started some food distribution, mainly cooking oil and de-germed corn meal—not the best of nutrition since almost all the protein had been removed from the corn. It was sad to see that displaced people had to make do with an inferior product from the USA. Later we saw some cases of pellagra due to a lack of Vitamin B.

It thrilled us to see people wanting to gather to thank God for their lives. Everybody had one or, more commonly, several family members or friends who had been killed up north. Although displaced to another province, they wanted to thank God together for their deliverance. At 7 A.M. every morning the church was packed out for thanksgiving services. In time, however, the enthusiasm and thankfulness wore off and slowly these services ceased.

There were multiple needs. For instance, many women did not have a change of clothes, having left Nyankunde and Bunia with nothing but the clothes on their backs. As these began to wear out we managed to buy enough material to make some 1500 wrap-around skirts. Not enough to meet the demand, but better than nothing. A seamstress found an old sewing machine, and we could pay her to hem up the lengths of cloth.

The hospital generously let us use some of its land to build housing for the medical staff from Nyankunde. Samaritan's Purse provided funds to buy timber and large rolls of blue plastic which were used to erect continuous rows of shacks under the supervision of the senior carpenter from Nyankunde. Although each family was only given a single room they could create some additional privacy inside through the judicious arrangement of further sheets of plastic. Thankfully we did not need to worry about heating or insulation, since it is warm all the time at the equator. However, the walkways between the rows would become very muddy after rain, and it was a battle to keep the rain from seeping in under the walls. At first young children had difficulty sleeping due to the light filtering through the plastic roofs; most Congolese houses have very small windows to discourage thieving, so are dark all the time. Samaritan's Purse thoughtfully provided enough funds so that we could build a larger construction in the middle of the camp that could be used as a church and community hall.

The nutritional needs of young children was another huge concern. Children need more protein than adults, and protein is expensive. Soya beans are an excellent source—there is more protein in a kilo of soya than in a kilo of beef. Soya grows very well in Congo, but it took some time before it was accepted into the local diet as it is more difficult to cook than regular beans (they need to be soaked for at least 12 hours before cooking). You can also grind soya beans into fine flour which can be added to other dishes.

We decided to arrange a breakfast club for young children. We organized the cooking of a huge vat of porridge consisting of 3/4 corn, ¼ soya flour, and a little sugar. To receive a plastic mug-full of porridge, each child had to bring a stick of firewood at least half their height. We'd use this wood to cook the next day's porridge.

Our main priority, however, was getting the nursing college up and running again. Over the next two months more and more students drifted in. For a reasonable price we managed to arrange housing for them in an old chief's compound. Oicha Hospital kindly let us use two rooms and an office. We were also able to use rooms at an existing nursing school in Oicha, as well as at a nearby rehabilitation center.

The first thing we did was organize exams, as the students had been forced out of Nyankunde just before the end-of-year could be arranged. We were amazed at the things people had carried with them on their 150 km walk through the jungle from Nyankunde. The office was set up using a small laptop which had survived the journey. Then various books from the Nyankunde libraries started showing up. When we started offering $5.- a book for "reimbursement of transport", their number increased remarkably. These were invaluable resources. We were even reunited with some of our personal books and effects, including my Canadian driving license.

Oicha was a busy general hospital, and it did not take long before we were fully involved with the medical work taking place there. While it was undergoing renovations I operated in a side room of the intensive care ward until they'd completed the new operating theatre. There were about 350 deliveries a month. Because of widespread malaria and stressful conditions, many mothers gave birth prematurely, so Nancy set up a small unit for underweight newborns which saved some very small babies.

Things were quiet for a couple of months. Then, in December 2002, considerable unrest broke out in Oicha. The rebels were thought to be coming down from the north, where our people had fled from to escape the fighting. Later we heard that the rebel soldiers had been promised $500 and a car each if they could take Beni, 29 km to the south of us. Our main source of news, the BBC, let us down completely at one stage, when it reported that Oicha had been attacked and the population displaced to Uganda. This was untrue, though it may have been what the rebels wanted. Nevertheless, people were very worried. Many locals fled, carrying a big roll of mattresses on their heads. No one really knew what to do: some set up camp in the fields outside of town while others left the countryside because they felt safer in town! At one point I went shopping for Nancy, and the small store where we normally purchased our groceries was completely empty. However the shopkeeper was there and asked what I wanted. I gave him a short list, and before long he had returned with everything I'd asked for.

Thankfully, the fighting never reached Oicha, although there was a heavy Congolese army presence. The turning point seemed to come in mid-December, when an important rebel leader was wounded and taken incognito to the Oicha hospital, where some of the Congolese soldiers recognized him and killed him in his bed.

Throughout all of this we kept very busy with our school and hospital duties. We had decided two months earlier that this is where we were supposed to be, and had not thought of evacuating again. Still, we were surprised that neither our own mission nor Mission Aviation

Fellowship asked if we wanted to leave. Some three months later, after things had quieted down, I met the town secretary of Oicha. "Good to meet you," he said. "I heard you were here. Your doctor (Dr. Kambale) came to see me just before Christmas and asked me what he should do with his whites. I told him to leave you where you were, that you'd be fine." He proved to be right, but I still don't understand how he could have had such an accurate assessment of the situation.

The Christmas service was held outside that year, because the church was too small to accommodate all who came. It was a beautiful sunny morning. Several choirs sang, and there was worship and preaching. Then, towards the end of the four hour service, we started hearing shooting off to the left. Suddenly a rebel ran right through the congregation. People began to panic and flee in all directions, trying to get to their houses as quickly as possible.

A second major influx of displaced people arrived in early January 2003 because of fighting in and around Bunia. They were initially housed in a primary school until further temporary housing could be arranged. Amazingly, we never had an epidemic of gastro-enteritis, although the population of Oicha had grown from 30,000 to 50,000.

No one had money, but some of the displaced people started collecting cast-off palm nuts. The stone in the middle of a kernel does not contain palm oil, so is usually discarded or burnt in the process of making oil. However, if you go to the trouble of cracking these very hard nuts you will find a small oily core that can be used to make soap. It is very labour-intensive, but some people managed to earn small amounts of money this way. The camps reverberated with the noise of stones cracking nuts.

We always appreciated it when short-term specialists came to help us expand and improve our services. Paul Bracken, who was brave enough to come from the UK to train two lab technicians to cut histology slides, also brought all the necessary equipment and chemicals with him. He had done the same thing at Nyankunde, but the lab with all its equipment there had been trashed. Dr. Jean Chamberlain then came to give seminars on maternal and child health care. One of her sessions was interrupted by gunfire, but we carried on as though nothing was happening. As was usual, we never learned the reason for that particular skirmish.

In May 2003 the town of Bunia suffered a fate similar to that of

Nyankunde. Of a population of around 200,000 only about 7000 remained in a United Nations compound set up in the middle of town. Everyone else fled into the surrounding countryside, with a number of them walking down to us in Oicha. Basically, the northern part of Bunia was at war with the southern part, and where they fought in the middle awful atrocities took place. The main weapon used was the machete, a large 60 cm heavy knife used to clear underbrush. People would die from partially amputated limbs or head wounds.

As I mentioned earlier, Nyankunde was closed for 1 ½ years. No one could live there because the area had been mined. Peace there was re-established in 2004 by a French "Artemis" force, after which the French transferred responsibility for the region to a force of some 17,000 UN troops. A South African detachment with sniffer dogs de-mined Nyankunde, and medical work could restart in April 2004.

In 2005 a final peace agreement was signed in the South African resort town of Sun City. The number of people killed during that decade of war in the Democratic Republic of Congo is generally now thought to be about 5.4 million, though it is not possible to confirm this figure with any accuracy. Some suggest that the real figure may only be half that. Either way, there was a terrific loss of life in a conflict largely ignored by the western media.

The Nyankunde medical complex sought to build on the peace process by allowing some of its members to establish a reconciliation program between the warring tribes. Invitations to come together for three days of seminars were sent to tribal elders and chiefs from the different warring parties. These seminars were built around the themes of mutual understanding and forgiveness. At one point the delegates were encouraged to write down the most horrific experience they had had during the war. Then they were invited to come forward and pin these pieces of paper onto an empty cross. Afterwards that cross was taken outside, and all the papers burnt in the center of a circle formed by the attendees, as a symbolic way of ridding themselves of their evil memories.

There were intense discussions at Oicha about the future of the Nyankunde Medical Center which, up to 2002, had been the largest medical facility in the north-east corner of Congo. Eventually the Executive Committee came to the decision that, instead of rebuilding it as it had been, it would be decentralized: two new, smaller institutions would be built, one to the north in Bunia and one to the south in Beni. Nyankunde itself would be rehabilitated as well. Some of those who had fled from Nyankunde had headed north to Bunia, while most had headed south to Oicha and Beni. A few people were interested in returning to Nyankunde. The group which had fled to Bunia ended up renting an old hotel in the centre of town, where they started a small hospital, while the group in Beni had rented an old coffee warehouse and started their own small hospital there. Rebuilding Nyankunde and building new hospitals in both Beni and Bunia would be very expensive indeed, but the teams were keen to trust God and give it a try.

All three projects have been largely completed with the help of TEAR Fund, Samaritan's Purse and a British organization called "Friends of CME", an organization set up by a former accountant at Nyankunde. TEAR Fund did not actually give money, but they gave us advice about where we could apply for grants and development funds. As a result we received funding from the Jersey Development Funds, Tear Holland, and many individuals and churches. Although we never solicited funds for our own personal finances, we have had no qualms about providing donor agencies with all the information they need for such capital projects as the rebuilding of hospitals.

The Nursing College was reestablished in its home province of Orientale in 2006, but had to be moved from Nyankunde to the much larger town of Bunia as most houses at Nyankunde had been demolished, and also because the College relies on a number of part time teachers, many of whom are from Bunia. Guildford Baptist Church paid for the first College building in Bunia, and then some individual members of the church enabled us to purchase the site on which the College now sits. Thanks to the input from the German charity 'Pain pour le Monde' the college boasts the best facilities of any college in north-eastern Congo, and possibly in the entire country. Two spacious amphitheatres hold 350 students each and 12 classrooms can each take up to 50 students. The Germans insisted on quality, and it shows!

And so it came to be that for a period of ten years we were involved in the administration of funds for a feeding program for displaced people in Oicha, the building of a classroom at the nursing school in Oicha, renovations at Nyankunde, two new hospitals in Bunia and Beni, and two schools for the deaf in Oicha and Bunia. How we praise God for prompting all the agencies and individuals involved for their generosity!

Now there are three functioning hospitals, one each in Beni, Bunia and Nyankunde working under the umbrella of the 'Centre Medical Evangelique'. This means that we have been able to serve our patients in the two big cities to the north and south of Nyankunde rather than waiting for them to come to us.

Things have changed dramatically since we first arrived in the Congo in 1973. Back then all the doctors and most of the nurses were expatriates. More recently, ourselves and Katsuko, a Japanese Lab Technician, were the only expatriates working at the Center. An increasing number of Congolese trained doctors come to us immediately after training for a 6 month internship.

Our biggest need is for some well trained specialists. In a city of some 300,000 people with a university and a faculty of medicine, we had, until recently, just eight specialists: one other surgeon, one ophthalmologist and five doctors who studied public health. Many doctors and some nurses undertake surgical operations because of the lack of specialists, but we are all distressed at the number of avoidable complications that this creates. We have sent doctors elsewhere in Africa for specialist training but two of the best trained have not wanted to return.

Excursion 10: The Sin of Indifference

Of the 38 parables Jesus told, 19 deal with handling possessions. They are not always easy to understand or apply—but then finance is a difficult subject. The parable at the beginning of Luke 16 pertains to the activities of a managerial crook.

This manager was a cunning, conniving, dishonest rascal-but you can't help but smile at his shrewdness. When he learned that he was about to lose his job because of dishonesty and mismanagement, he went to the boss' best customers and gave them deep discounts on what they owed. This opened the way for him to go to one of those customers who now "owed him a favor" in the hope of getting a job. When he was fired even his boss commended him: "I've got to hand it to you, you cunning, devious, despicable fellow-just my kind of guy-now get out of my sight!"

Jesus encourages Christians to be more savvy in the ways of the world—but without becoming like it. Sadly, Christians can be the most gullible, naïve folks around. In this parable Jesus taught four practical principles about handling money.

1. Your best investment is in people that you'll see in Heaven, rather than in things (Luke 16:9): "I tell you, use worldly wealth to gain friends for yourselves, so that when it is gone, you will be welcomed into eternal dwellings." The medical infrastructure that we have been involved in in the Congo has been destroyed twice in the last 50 years, first in the Simba rebellion and then in what we now call Africa's First World War. These events reinforced our focus on teaching and equipping. Sure, we need buildings, but the more important priority is leaving a legacy of active Christian medical workers prepared to give a lifetime of service.

2. The way you manage God's money determines if He can trust you with true riches (vs. 10-12) Jesus said, "Whoever can be trusted with very little can also be trusted with much, and whoever is dishonest with very little will also be dishonest with much. So if you have not been trustworthy in handling worldly wealth, who will trust you with true riches? And if you have not been trustworthy with someone else's property, who will give you property of your own?" We need to entrust people at the start of their careers with simple tasks to see how they do. Based on that we can gradually trust them with greater things.

    Jesus mentions two kinds of wealth in this passage. Firstly he speaks of "worldly wealth", or the money God entrusts us to manage. All the wealth in the world belongs to God, and He gives us some of it with which to buy the basics to meet our needs (he never promised to meet our wants). Secondly, Jesus speaks of something he called "true riches." If you prove to be trustworthy with worldly wealth, God can trust you with true riches. True riches have nothing to do with money. They include spiritual blessings like peace, security, and fortitude—things so valuable they can't be bought at any price.

3. Money is a great servant but a terrible master (Luke 16:13). "No servant can serve two masters. Either he will hate the one and love the other, or he will be devoted to the one and despise the other. You

cannot serve both God and Money." The word "Mammon" is an Aramaic word the translators of the Authorized Version chose not to translate, since they thought it was the proper name of a demon, the pagan god of riches. Today we understand it to refer simply to worldly wealth or money, and this seems to best fit the context. It has been said that money is like salt water: the more you drink it, the thirstier you become—and the more you want to drink.

4. While money is temporary, God's Word and "true wealth" are forever (Luke 16:14-18). One day money will disappear, possibly in a huge worldwide financial catastrophe just prior to Jesus' second coming. There will be no money in heaven—that is why it is called "worldly wealth". The story is told of a man who received permission to take his most prized possession to heaven. When St. Peter looked into his bag and saw the huge slab of gold the man was carrying he said, "Oh, a paving stone...!"

You cannot take "worldly wealth" with you, but you can send it on ahead. Jesus spoke about "laying up treasures in heaven". This could mean investing our money in people, because people have eternal souls and can go to heaven. Philippians 4:1 refers to those we have helped as "our crowns". However, Jesus is pointing to something else that is eternal, the Word of God. There are only two things of eternal value in this world: people's souls and God's Word. Those are the two things we should invest in...

All of us need to make up our minds with respect to the subject of money. Is it good, bad or neutral? Beyond doubt, the love of money, craving it, is a huge problem (I Timothy 6:9-10). But why can it lead us astray so easily? We invented the stuff but seem incapable of managing it well.

After documenting Jesus' instruction about money, Luke records the parable he told about a poor beggar, Lazarus by name, and a rich man who remains anonymous (Luke 16:10). The name "Lazarus" is the Greek equivalent of the Hebrew name "Eleazar", which means "God is my helper". We can assume that Jesus wanted us to understand that—unlike the rich man—Lazarus trusted in God. An enormous economic gulf separated the two men during their lives here on earth. Lazarus, constantly hungry, looked longingly at the pieces of bread the rich man's guests used to feed the dogs. Furthermore, Lazarus was ill, but could not afford bandages for the open sores covering his body, his ulcers attracting flies and dogs. Although the rich man knew Lazarus personally, as indicated by the fact that he referred to him by name, there is no indication he ever gave him anything.

After their respective deaths, a different gulf separated the two men. Their positions had reversed—and the change was fixed for eternity! Neither could ever cross to the other's side... The rich man, though guilty of ignoring Lazarus, was not accused of being the cause of his misery. There is no hint of exploitation—just of indifference. He had merely acquiesced to a situation of dehumanizing economic inequality.

When it was too late to redeem himself the rich man begged to have Lazarus go warn his five brothers, who were as bound for hell as he had been. What would these brothers have thought if the ragged, dirty Lazarus returned from the dead to tell them he'd been dispatched by their brother to urge them to start living upright, God centered lives? They'd have been even more incredulous than Israel's religious and political authorities were when they heard that Jesus had risen from the dead. Soon afterwards Jesus really did restore to life a dead man named Lazarus. Although many believed in Jesus because of this dramatic miracle, not all of its results were beneficial. Israel's religious elite became more determined than ever to get rid of the evidence, and to have both Lazarus and Jesus put to death (John 11:53, 12:10).

Had the Lazarus of Jesus' story, the poor beggar, been able to return to earth, his message would undoubtedly have been that we should all be compassionate toward the poor! He would have taught that the possession of wealth necessitates accepting responsibility for the poor. But we must look deeper: are the economic and spiritual differences which Jesus describes in this parable related? Is it really because of his wealth that the rich man went to hell, and because of his poverty that Lazarus went to heaven? Did simple economics decide their fate? Or was it their use or misuse of money that was the determining factor in their destiny?

As mentioned, Lazarus' name indicates that he trusted God and had a living relationship with Him, and it was this relationship, and not the lack of wealth, that determined his eternal destiny. At the same time, however, his social condition may have been instrumental in generating that relationship. His ill health and lack of resources were daily reminders of his need for divine help. He may have called out to others, like the rich man, for help and, having been refused time and again, finally turned to God. And although God did not bless him materially in this life, He gave him something even better: eternal communion with Himself, in a perfect place, with a perfect spirit and a perfect body, for all of eternity. God's modus operandi is to take something bad and work it into something good.

The deciding factor in the rich man's eternal destiny pertained to the nature of his relationship with God. His self-sufficiency may have influenced his decision not to obey God. Many wealthy people feel they have "need of nothing", and certainly not God. What would a sports star or Hollywood actor need God for, when every single one of their temporal needs is amply fulfilled? This, however, is exactly the point. Their need is not a temporal one but rather a spiritual one. The rich man was wealthy in material goods, but spiritually broke. By neglecting his relationship with God, or by deciding that he didn't need Him, he either consciously or unconsciously headed down a path which led away from the Creator and towards a godless life. And when he eventually entered eternity, God gave him exactly what he had wanted all along: life without Him.

It is possible that, in spite of his riches, there were moments in his earthly life when the rich man experienced a foretaste of what he was now experiencing in his afterlife, namely that life without God can be hellish. But his heart had become either so flabby or so hardened that he didn't respond to those epiphanies which God mercifully sends. He persisted in living without God.

11

Retirement

AFTER MOST of a lifetime in the wilderness of Africa, retirement loomed. We eventually decided that central Toronto, close to our main Canadian supporting church, would be the ideal place to sink some roots—if we could ever afford to do so! Our meager retirement savings were nowhere near enough to purchase an apartment in that expensive city. Then, in 2005, an elderly aunt in the UK died and left her apartment to her four nieces and nephews. My three siblings, who each owned their own homes, were generous enough to give us the apartment. They received the rental income until we were finally ready to retire in 2010.

Once the UK apartment had been sold we knew how much money we had to spend. We instructed a real estate agent to find a two-bedroom apartment close to the church. "Sorry," came the reply. "there is only one property that fits those requirements."

"No need to be sorry! We only want to buy one apartment!" We went to see it, and moved in three weeks later. The Lord was not finished providing for us yet. One of our Toronto-based supporters realized that we would need a car, and bought us a brand new Honda—the first time we ever owned a new car. Thank you, Lord!

We had been warned not to say "yes" to too many invitations in retirement. I wasn't sure there would be any, but many interesting doors have opened to us in the heart of this vibrant multicultural city. There is plenty to do, much of it linked to our African service. We are so grateful for everything. I thank the Lord each morning for water and electricity, two things we never take for granted.

During our forty years in Africa we witnessed amazing changes. We began as part of a large expatriate community, during a time when all doctors and many of the nurses were missionaries. We were thrilled to get our first African doctor, Dr. Jo Lusi, to whom in the course of time (and with a certain amount of pressure from him) we could start paying a reasonable salary. When I became Medical Director of the center, he followed me as head of the nursing school and then, in 1987, he became medical director. I am convinced that the gradual changeover from missionary to national was of God. The fact that Dr. Lusi's wife was British, and an ex-missionary, made them a wonderful bridging couple.

The nationalization of the medical center happened in part because missionaries were advised to leave during the war. Most did not return. Although one would hardly wish war on anyone, there were a number of positive consequences in which we see God's hand. In the first place, we were forced to hand over leadership and responsibility to our African colleagues. This was not easy for them, as some of them had very limited educational backgrounds. Today, however, our best leaders have received their higher education outside of the country. The director of the nursing college has a PhD from Liege, Belgium—even though the Congolese diaspora in Belgium urged him to stay there: "Why would you want to go back to Congo? Life is much easier here!" He is doing a marvelous job organizing the graduate and masters programs.

However, we have to reflect very carefully about who we can sponsor for further education in Europe—or even elsewhere in Africa—as many do not return. We sent a very gifted doctor to Malawi for Orthopedic training. Upon graduation he decided to stay in Malawi, where life is much easier than in unsettled Congo.

Unfortunately, medical education in Congo leaves a lot to be desired. If you have a high school diploma and can find the academic fees for six years of medical studies you will find a medical college that will accept you. The university is pleased to receive the fees, and the more students they enroll the easier it is to run the university. Grading such large numbers of exam papers then becomes an impossible task, as is finding well-supervised practical experience. We have established a scholarship program to enable a select few to get broader experience elsewhere in Africa before they take up leadership roles. We hope that these people will, in the future, be able to organize specialist training programs in country.

How can I justify the repeated short-term visits we make to the Congo since our "retirement" if we believe that the Lord forced us to nationalize the medical work there? The easy answer is that we constantly receive warm invitations to return. We trust that our visits are a source of encouragement, and that any advice given may prove to be useful, even if not given from a position of leadership. Having said that, I sometimes wonder if a total withdrawal of foreign expertise would force the country to work out its own, ongoing problems of political mismanagement, security and financial corruption...

The other major benefit of the war at Nyankunde was the fact that it forced the work to decentralize, which led to the establishment of three hospitals in the place of one.

Excursion 11: Eternity Can Be Lonely

Luke reports Jesus saying, "It is more blessed to give than to receive" (Acts 20:35). This story has focused on the amazing ways God has given to us, but Luke reminds us that we should be giving just as we receive. How should we go about that?

Give generously, whether out of your plenty or out your poverty. Luke describes how Jesus once watched the rich putting their gifts into the temple treasury. Then he noticed a poor widow put in two very small copper coins. "I tell you the truth," he said, "this poor widow has put in more than all the others. All these people gave their gifts out of their wealth; but she out of her poverty put in all she had to live on" (Luke 21:1-4). People who give sacrificially realize, of course, that they worked hard for what they take home, but they also know that God blessed them and provided for them. They are not only socially secure in Jesus, they are spiritually secure in Him as well. They can trust Him with their money. Jesus commended the poor widow because she gave everything. Everything!

However, we cannot outgive God. In Luke 14:33 Jesus states, "So, therefore, whoever of you does not renounce all that he has cannot be my disciple." Later, in Luke 18:28, where Peter boasted that "Behold, we have left all, and followed thee." Jesus responded, saying, "No one who has left home or wife or brothers or parents or children for the sake of the kingdom of God will fail to receive many times as much in this age, and in the age to come, eternal life" (Luke 18:29,30).

I cannot say that I have given up everything for Christ. For one thing,

I retained my calling as a doctor, while the disciples gave up their careers as fishermen or tax collectors. On the other hand, I have learned to hold the material things of this world lightly, particularly since almost all of it was stolen from us on that fateful September 5, 2002. Since then my life has been marvelously rich in terms of having a fulfilling ministry and in being a channel for the Lord to provide some of the funds needed to resurrect one hospital and to build two others, as well as a nursing college.

When we first left for Africa, our friends and family questioned why one would ever go there after receiving our kind of education. Now we hear them commenting that we "seem to have had a very interesting career!" Well, one thing is sure: we have been wonderfully satisfied with good things. Now we have just one further ambition, and that is to encourage others to make similar radical career choices as they are directed by God.

Money may be one of the least-discussed topics in the church today. True, there are plenty of exhortations to stewardship along with periodic drives for fund-raising, but few preachers or teachers are prepared to systematically tackle a theology of money. Few dare to look carefully at what Jesus taught about the subject of finance, and it is difficult to find good books on the topic even though Jesus had more to say about it than on almost anything else! Well he might, seeing the great power money has over most of our lives. In his parables Jesus often contrasts money with relationships, suggesting that we will get far more pleasure from our association with others than we get from wealth.

Luke 15 tells the story of two brothers, both of whom seemed to have plenty of money, and neither of whom had real friends. The younger son ran from home and used up his inheritance in riotous living. But when the money ran out his friends deserted him. They loved him for what he could give them, not for who he was. As for the older brother who slaved away to increase his inheritance—it is hard to escape the nasty suspicion that he had plenty of cash but no friends.

In one sense we are all heading for bankruptcy. We will die and have to leave everything behind. It is said that after John D. Rockefeller died someone asked how much he left behind. "Everything," was the terse reply. The Arabs have a saying: a shroud has no pockets. All of us will, one day, have to take leave of everything. Will we then have any friends? Are we using our present possessions to form good relationships?

According to an Albanian proverb, those who eat alone will die alone...

Seeing things in the light of eternity makes it all different. How many people will welcome you into eternity when you die? The way we spend our money may be an indication of what faces us after we pass into eternity, when all will be revealed. Money spent helping people get to heaven is money invested in eternity, it equals eternal riches. Use your money to make friends in heaven. If you only make friends here on earth you will face a long and lonely eternity.

12

To Conclude...

FEW WOULD dispute that western society is extremely individualistic and that it encourages a selfish approach to life. Christians are called to be prophetic voices. We must speak out as well as provide fresh insights into the different aspects of life—and money.

The reaction of the rich young ruler we met in Luke 18 suggests that Jesus advised people to be rather radical. You, who are able and can afford to read this book, are among the world's richest people in purely monetary terms. Yet most of those who fall into this category don't realize that they are poor, miserable and blind with respect to the deeper aspects of life, and particular in terms of eternal values (Revelation 3:17).

God presents us with the opportunity to invest in things which offer much greater returns than any earthly investment. To be able to take advantage of that opportunity, however, we have to believe that God is a giver, not a taker. And if He moves you to give up your all, it is only because that all is but a microcosm of the macrocosm of riches He wishes to bestow upon us.

The rich young ruler left sadly. He still had all his money, but he had short-changed himself. Jesus, too, felt sad as he watched him walk away from the much better riches He had offered him. It was a tragedy of epic proportions which, sadly, is repeated every time a person fails to exercise complete faith in God's provision. There are few big businessmen in the church

C.T. Studd, the founder of WEC International, once said "A man is no fool to give up what he cannot keep to gain what he cannot lose." You cannot live for both money and God – one or the other must come first. We worship God and we make money. Deep down we think wealth is God's blessing and poverty a curse. Jesus taught that God's take on the matter is different. In His way of thinking wealth is often a curse and poverty a blessing (Luke 6:20).

Jesus was rich, but for our sake he became poor so that through his poverty we might become rich for eternity (2 Cor. 8:9). The church struggles in affluent countries while it grows in the poor and troubled parts of the world. For example, in the rich world divorce is all too common. It is one of the marks of an affluent society because when you have money you buy what you want and take the liberty to discard what you don't want. Write it off and make another contract.

I have been wrestling with money management ever since I started living on that exciting, beautiful, but financially impoverished and mismanaged continent of Africa. Although I have no easy answers, I trust I have managed to pose some important questions. I spend many hours in the West trying to manage my money and my financial affairs— running the danger of having it managing me, and dictating the choices I have to make in life.

The job of the Old Testament prophet was to analyze his society to understand the direction in which it was being pushed. Then he was to wave one of two flags - green or red - to either encourage or warn of the necessity for an about-face. They were generally not well-received because their messages were mostly of red-flag variety. They acquired a very negative image because much of their time was spent encouraging the community of believers to resist the cultural norms of their time.

Jesus was much more than a prophet, yet He was also that *par excellence*. His insights into society enabled Him to give radical solutions to the cultural pressures of his day. Some of those pressures have changed somewhat since his time. For instance, today we live in an era of "political correctness" in the Western world which, on the one hand, can help inculcate respect for human rights and environmental concerns but, on the other hand, suggests that there is only one correct answer to each particular problem. And the answer generally given tends to be simplistic. How else can you channel unthinking people towards a single opinion? The prevailing attitude conveyed by our culture today is that solutions come when you throw money at the problem. That is not the Christian way.

In closing, let me summarize the main ideas I have learnt from the life and teachings of Jesus:

1. The alternative to a "money first" approach to life is the "relationships first" approach. Jesus emphasized the truth that relationships are much more important than money. We must work out how, as social beings, we can develop healthy relationships within families and with friends. We need to build lasting relationships to give our lives spice and vigor. We recognize that money is deceptive in this area. Change in my priorities with regard to the way we spend our time can help start in this process of reorientation from money to relationships.

2. Great blessing results from a generous attitude towards others. We must be generous not only with our money, but with all the gifts, attributes, time and resources that God has given us to manage. He knows that we are most contented when we focus our love to Him and towards our fellow men as opposed to ourselves.

3. The secret to a relaxed attitude to life rests in a deepening trust and commitment to God. For many, life in the twenty first century is hectic. With God's help we need to learn to cope with the stress, anxiety, even panic, which contemporary life can breed. An understanding of the believer's position in Christ, and the resources that our heavenly Father puts at our disposal is the cure that Jesus offers for this insidious modern malady.

4. The importance of simplifying our lifestyles. Simplifying my busy life taught me that it really is possible "to live more with less". All our labor-saving devices do not seem to have left us with more free time than our ancestors had. Everyone complains about the busyness of life. Every American adult (over 15) spends an average of 2.8 hours a day in front of the television.[8] This, of course, discourages analytical thinking and erodes the ability to concentrate, and seems to result in an adult-type of attention-deficit disorder. This means that we need constant entertainment, whether at home, school, church or work. Jesus advocated a radical simplification of His disciples' lifestyles.

5. We must make deliberate, well thought-through choices when setting our financial goals and priorities. How can we make the money entrusted

---

[8] Bureau of Labor Statistics: American time use survey 2014.

to us really count for something in today's world? This means weighing up alternatives carefully, and investing in worthwhile enterprises. We can invest with a view to maximizing immediate personal monetary gain, or we can think carefully about how we can best invest in Christ's kingdom.

6. We must debunk the myth of the advantages of financial independence, the myth that holds that it is possible to guarantee one's financial security. Conventional wisdom suggests that ultimate happiness comes when we are financially independent, and thus free to cater to our every whim. Jesus taught that happiness is not possible outside of a whole-hearted reliance on the Creator. It happens when the sustainer of this universe becomes the cornerstone of our lives.

7. We must recognize that we will face shortages. What happens when all this advice, this trust that God will provide what we need, does not seem to work? Have we misunderstood, misbehaved, or in some other way missed the help God has provided—or do we, in fact, already have all we need? The particular challenges we face may demand that we use our present resources more efficiently, while not failing to communicate more with God when we are in need.

8. We must consider renouncing wealth as a real option. We are constantly told that we could make a fortune by purchasing a lottery ticket or investing in the stock market. The unlikely advice that Jesus gave a young man who was on the way up was to sell all he had and start following Him.

St. Peter, the disciples' spokesperson, defied the accepted patterns of his day in both word and action, and encourages us to do the same. He urges us to "live as strangers and aliens in the world" (1 Peter 2:11). A non-conformist to the end, tradition tells us that he asked to be crucified upside down when he was about to be executed. That kind of non-conformity can make us uncomfortable—but that is what prophets should be doing! Their calling is to tear away the disguises we make for ourselves and behind which we hide in order to expose our selfishness.

So let us press on to know the LORD!

Philip Wood is a British born surgeon who has worked most of his professional life in the heart of Africa.

His priority has been teaching and encouraging young Africans in good and appropriate medical care. This priority came at first from personal conviction, then political necessity and more recently at the instigation of the national church.

Philip has written 2 previous books and numerous scientific articles.

He now lives with his wife Nancy in Toronto, Canada.

Printed in Great Britain
by Amazon